ROY JOHNSTON on his retirement fro
himself free to indulge a lifelong musical h
the Arts Council of Northern Ireland an
committee, a member of the Governors of t
board of Castleward Opera, and a trustee o
some years of writing, lecturing and broa
history he wrote a dissertation on 'Concerts
1874' for which Queen's University awarded him a doctorate in 1996, and which he has drawn on in 'Bunting's Messiah'.

Etching of Bunting as an old man,
from Petrie's article in the *Dublin University Magazine* of January 1847

To John + Audrey
with best wishes,
Roy

BUNTING'S *Messiah*

ROY JOHNSTON

THE BELFAST NATURAL HISTORY
AND PHILOSOPHICAL SOCIETY
IN ASSOCIATION WITH
ULSTER HISTORICAL FOUNDATION

THE BELFAST NATURAL HISTORY AND PHILOSOPHICAL SOCIETY, founded in 1821, encourages understanding of the human and natural environment of Ireland, both past and present. It has a particular focus on Belfast and its hinterland. It promotes original scholarship, and new ideas and interpretations, which are of an academic standard and yet are accessible to a wider audience.

First published 2003
by the Belfast Natural History and Philosophical Society,
c/o the Linen Hall Library,
17 Donegall Square North, Belfast BT1 5GD
in association with Ulster Historical Foundation
12 College Square East, Belfast BT1 6DD

Distributed by Ulster Historical Foundation

ISBN 0-9539604-6-3

Printed by ColourBooks Ltd., Ireland
Design by Dunbar Design

To

David Byers,

for many years of friendship

and encouragement

CONTENTS

LIST OF ILLUSTRATIONS

ACKNOWLEDGEMENTS

For permission to use and quote from essential sources in their care, or of which they own the copyright, I thank the following:

Amber Adams
David Byers
Queen's University Library, Special Collections
The Linen Hall Library
The Ulster Museum
The Public Record Office of Northern Ireland
The National Gallery, Dublin and
The National Portrait Gallery, London

My thanks are due also to the Belfast Natural History and Philosophical Society who commissioned this essay, and to Fintan Mullan of the Ulster Historical Foundation, Angélique Day, Amber Adams and Wendy Dunbar for their advice and positive help in getting it into print.

No. 44. CHORUS.—HALLELUJAH!

INTRODUCTION

IT IS THE HARPERS' FESTIVAL OF 1792 which gives Belfast its own place in the history of music. In that seminal event an important role was filled by the nineteen-year-old Edward Bunting, and under its stimulus he went on to initiate and expand researches of his own. They formed the basis of a lifelong study of the greatest importance in the conservation, critical study and dissemination of a major traditional music. The present-day enlargement of the scope of musical studies, aided by the breadth of research made accessible by sophisticated methods of discovery and communication, has enhanced the importance of the study of traditional music, and confirmed the stature of Edward Bunting within it.

Bunting's own musicianship, and his training in the mainstream European music of his day, were necessary attributes. In the present age of cultural relativism and 'world music', 'mainstream' is an epithet to be applied with caution, if at all. In the latter half of the eighteenth century, however, the ethnic musics of Europe were only beginning to be explored, and the musics of other continents, if known at all, were regarded as barbaric. European art music, with that of Italy and Germany predominating, was the accepted music of Europe and the Europeanised parts of the world, a musical *lingua franca* based on a common tonality which transcended boundaries. To refer to it as the mainstream music of Bunting's day is a simple historical statement of fact, and it is so used in this essay. His training in this musicianship enabled him to make a transcription of the traditional music he heard and to work on it. It also fulfilled the necessary function of providing him with a living. His three volumes of what he called the 'ancient music' brought him fame but not fortune.[1] Not qualified to make a living otherwise, he was a working professional musician all his life.

It would be expected of a professional musician that he would be a competent player of his instrument or instruments, that he would be able to teach them to others, and that he would have a working knowledge of them in terms of construction, tuning and repair. Bunting's capability went further. He had a performing skill on organ, harpsichord and piano that attracted praise beyond Belfast. He developed skills in the new (to Belfast) field of concert promotion, the highlights of which were his attraction to Belfast of the soprano Angelica Catalani and his organisation of a four-day festival in the course of which Handel's *Messiah* was given its first full Belfast performance. The distinctive character and growth of the town of that day offered musical challenges; the response to them of Bunting and of other musicians, in particular his master William Ware, assisted and shaped the growth of a Belfast musical public. Edward Bunting would have had a significant place in the history of music in Belfast if the harpers' festival had never taken place and he had never been involved in the 'ancient music'.

Studies of the reception of music and the growth of a musical public in the provincial towns have found a place in the social history of music, which is now well established in its own right as an academic discipline, with its own contribution to make to the study and enjoyment of music through placing it in its social context. Applied as it has been to the social history of music in Belfast, it has enabled the role of Edward Bunting in the reception of the European mainstream music of his day to be examined and his stature as a musician enhanced in a further dimension. The purpose of this esssay is to consider in detail his career in the years when he worked in Belfast as a professional musician, and in so doing to place him in the social and musical world of his time.

NOTE

1 Bunting published the results of his researches in three volumes, in 1796, 1809 and 1840. They are referred to in this essay as BUNTING 1796, BUNTING 1809 and BUNTING 1840; for their full titles see Bibliography.

1

PRELUDE

'WANTED,

An Apprentice from the age of nine to twelve, by William Ware, Organist of St Ann's church, Belfast. A Fee is required. None need apply who cannot be well recommended, and who has not a Taste for the Musical Profession'.

Belfast News-Letter,
28 September–2 October 1781

EDWARD BUNTING WROTE COPIOUSLY about traditional music in his letters and notebooks and in his three published volumes, but he wrote very little about his activities in the mainstream music of his day, and even less about his own life. For his years in Belfast there is fortunately a good deal of contemporary source material, mostly but not entirely in the newspapers. For the eleven years of his life before he came to Belfast no contemporary sources have yet come to light. In default of contemporary information, those who have written about Bunting's early life, up to and including Moloney,[1] have relied on two sources. One is a substantial valedictory article on him which appeared in a Dublin magazine in 1847, three years after Bunting died.[2] The article is signed 'P', and internal evidence makes it clear that this is George Petrie (1790–1866), who also made an important collection of traditional music, following, not uncritically, in the footsteps of his subject. The other is Charlotte Milligan Fox's book on the Irish harpers.[3] Presumably because it was aimed at the general reader of its day, it includes very little scholarly apparatus; it acknowledges some but by no means all of its sources, there are very few footnotes and no bibliography. This is a pity, because it is plain that Fox had access to a good deal of source material. For Bunting's early years she quotes copiously from Petrie, adding only a little of her own (sources unacknowledged).

Edward Bunting's father, we gather, was a Derbyshire engineer who came to the north of Ireland, married and settled there.[4] His wife, says Petrie,

> was the lineal descendant of a certain chief of an ancient clan … seated in Tyrone, named Para, or Patrick Gruana O'Quin, who was killed in arms in July 1642; and it was to this origin that Bunting attributed his musical talents.[5]

There were three sons, Anthony (born 29 November 1765), John (born in 1776), and Edward, born at Armagh in February 1773.[6] Fox says all three 'were trained by Barnes, then organist there'.[7] If she means that they were pupils of Robert Barnes while he was organist of St Patrick's cathedral, this requires modification. Barnes, according to one authority, was appointed to Armagh in 1759.[8] Another does not mention Barnes, and gives Dr Langrishe Doyle as organist appointed in that year.[9] A further authority says that Primate Robinson, in his restructuring of the choir in 1776, replaced Robert Barnes as 'insufficient' by 'a good organist' and demoted him to vicar choral.[10] It is most unlikely that Edward Bunting, three years old in 1776, would have been taught by Barnes. Perhaps his brothers were; but the better fortune, one feels, would have been for all three to have been pupils of Langrishe Doyle, who left Armagh to become organist of the two cathedrals of Dublin, Christ Church and St Patrick's, where he was to preside for thirty-four years in the most prestigious post in the Irish anglican church. His successor in Armagh, Richard Langdon, did not take up the post until 1782. Langdon may not have encountered Edward Bunting, for, according to Petrie,

> at a very early age he had the misfortune to lose his father, who left him unprovided for; and at the age of nine, having already shown a decided predilection for music, he was removed to Drogheda, where his eldest brother Anthony … was then located as a music teacher

> and organist. Here he remained for two years, during which he received musical instruction from his brother.[11]

Both Petrie and Fox are silent on the circumstances of the father's death which left the seventeen-year-old Anthony with the upbringing of his brother, and on whether their mother had died by then or, if widowed, what became of her. Petrie goes on:

> [he] made such progress in his art, that his fame spread to Belfast, whither, at the age of eleven, he proceeded, at the invitation of Mr Weir [*sic*], then organist of the church there, to take his place at the instrument, while that gentleman made a visit to London. It was very soon discovered at Belfast that the boy substitute was a better organist than his employer and Mr Weir was glad to secure his services as assistant, by articles, for a limited number of years. While thus engaged he had, in addition to his duties as assistant or sub-organist at the church, to act also as deputy teacher to Mr Weir's pupils on the pianoforte, throughout the neighbouring country.[12]

Petrie names no sources of his information, and it is a fair guess that what he says about Bunting's early life may have come from Bunting himself, for they were friends. They did not meet, however, until some unspecified time after the appearance of Bunting's second collection (published 1809), and Bunting's recollections may have been those of a man in his forties and quite possibly a good deal older. The 'spread of his fame', the seeking of his services by the Belfast organist, the discovery that he was the better organist, all smack of a man remembering 'with advantages'.

No indication of response to the advertisement quoted at the head of this chapter appears, and it does not seem to have been repeated. In 1781 Edward Bunting had not reached the lower age limit of the advertisement and had not yet gone to Drogheda. It seems likely that this was the post to which he was appointed three years later, the 'fee' presumably paid by his brother Anthony, who may indeed have negotiated the post with Ware, another Armagh alumnus. Not for the last time in this essay one regrets the inability to consult William Ware's cash book; an invaluable source, it was available to earlier writers on Belfast and has now disappeared. Whatever clouds of juvenile glory Edward Bunting was trailing, in reality or in fallacious memory, and whatever designation – assistant, sub-organist – he attached to it, it is most likely that it was as an articled apprentice that he entered the service of William Ware.

For his regular career as a working musician in Belfast, only lightly touched on in Petrie and Fox, there is available a good deal of contemporary source material. Those parts which had to do with public concerts, and formed his major contribution to the musical life of Belfast, were lived in public, and thus attracted the attention of the newspapers. Newspaper coverage is not the only contemporary source, but it is much the largest. There are also non-contemporary sources, in which however the tendency to see personalities and events of former centuries with the eyes of the writer's own can lead occasionally to what may be called retrospective elevation; examples will appear.

NOTES

1 COLETTE MOLONEY, *The Irish music manuscripts of Edward Bunting (1773–1843): an introduction and catalogue* (Dublin, Irish Traditional Music Archive, 2000).
2 'Our portrait gallery. No XLI – Edward Bunting. With an etching,' *Dublin University Magazine*, XXIX (clxix), January 1847, pp. 64–73.
3 CHARLOTTE MILLIGAN FOX, *The Annals of the Irish Harpers* (London, Smith, Elder, 1911).
4 FOX, *Annals*, p. 10, says he came from the town of Shottle at the opening of mines at Coalisland, described by PETRIE, *Bunting*, p. 66, as the Dungannon Colliery. Fox's attribution of a birthplace may rest on a copy of the will, dated 14 August 1759, of an Anthony Bunting, then living in London, who names among the beneficiaries George, Samuel and William Bunting 'now or late of Shottle in the county of Derby': *Bunting MSS*, 4/35/38. The copyist does not, however, offer it as absolute proof that this is Edward Bunting's family.
5 PETRIE, *Bunting*, p. 67.
6 PETRIE, *Bunting*, p. 67.
7 FOX, *Annals*, p. 11.
8 ALOIS FLEISCHMANN (ed.), *Music in Ireland: a symposium* (Cork, Cork University Press and Oxford, Blackwell, 1952), p.162.
9 W.H. GRINDLE, *Irish cathedral music: a history of music at the cathedrals of the Church of Ireland* (Institute of Irish Studies, Queen's University, Belfast, 1989), p. 219.
10 JOE MCKEE, *The choral foundation of Armagh Cathedral 1600–1870* (unpublished MA thesis, Queen's University, Belfast, 1982), pp. 310–311.
11 PETRIE, *Bunting*, p. 67.
12 PETRIE, *Bunting*, p. 67.

2
BELFAST IN 1784

'From the year 1770 to the period of the legislative union with Great Britain, the remarkable nature of the information for compiling a history of Belfast is only equalled by its copiousness. The desire of scrutinising into public affairs seems to have gathered strength from the increase of commerce; and in those numerous discussions which the events of Europe or the state of the nation so loudly and so frequently called forth, this town was always the first and the boldest in the declaration of its sentiments.'

GEORGE BENN,
The History of the Town of Belfast (Belfast, Mackay, 1823),
pp. 49–50

PHYSICAL APPEARANCE

EDWARD BUNTING HAD SPENT HIS LIFE SO FAR in two towns. Armagh, the site of a church of St Patrick's since the fifth century, had a long and important history, ecclesiastical and political, and was the site of the cathedral of the arch-diocese of the anglican church in Ireland and the official home of its primate. Drogheda, a Norse foundation, had been one of the most important English towns in medieval Ireland, the site of several parliaments and in later centuries a place much fought over in the English civil war and the Williamite wars. Belfast was quite unlike either. By the time Bunting arrived in

Belfast in 1784, Armagh had amassed a population in excess of 2,000,[1] but that of Belfast had advanced from less than 700 to 15,000 in little more than a century. In the course of this rapid growth it had become the principal export outlet for the agricultural produce of a substantial hinterland, trading not only with Britain but with France and what had been the American colonies. Urban improvement lagged behind its mercantile expansion to an extent that led a noble neighbour, Lord Massereene, to describe it in 1752 as 'in a ruinous condition, likely to lose both its Trade and Inhabitants if it is not speedily supported by proper Tenures'.[2] Belfast was part of the lands of the Chichester family, the earls of Donegall. After their Jacobean castle in Belfast was accidentally burnt down in 1708 (the site commemorated today by such place names as Castle Place and Castle Street), the family left Belfast and dwelt in England for the remainder of the eighteenth century. The fifth earl, who inherited in 1757, did a good deal for the urban profile of the town. The great majority of his new leases imposed obligations on the lessees to build, to a greater height and with a higher standard of materials; houses had to be twenty-eight feet high in Castle Place and twenty-five in High Street.[3] A new market house was put up in 1769 on a new site at the Four Corners at the earl's expense. Two years later two important foundation stones were laid, both in the new street which bore the family name, Donegall Street. The Charitable Society's Poor House was opened in 1774 on land donated by the earl. Two years later a new parish church, St Anne's, was provided. By that time also the earl had added an upper floor to the new market house, for which he called in a first-class London architect, Robert Taylor,

> one of the last and greatest of the English Palladians … Architect of the King's Works, and shortly to be knighted … The interior … was very splendid for a provincial market town, with a vaulted and coffered ceiling, Corinthian pilasters, and ornamental plasterwork foreshadowing the designs of the Adams brothers.[4]

As the Exchange Rooms, they provided the town with a business and social centre, and a concert room of superior amenity. There were other new buildings in which the earl was not involved. First Presbyterian Church in Rosemary Street, by Roger Mulholland, was opened in 1783. In the following year no less than three further

John Nixon's watercolour of High Street in 1786
PRIVATE COLLECTION

public buildings came into operation: St Mary's in Chapel Lane, the first Roman Catholic church in the town; the White Linen Hall, on a site provided by the earl where the City Hall now stands; and Michael Atkins' theatre in Rosemary Lane. Armagh and Drogheda had not been without new construction, but the Belfast which greeted the young Edward Bunting had been transformed, in the look of its streets and their houses, and in its public buildings, none of which, with the exception of the old market house, was more than ten years old. Bunting on arrival would have seen High Street as it was when John Nixon made his well-known watercolour in the spring of 1786.

All the buildings in that view had been recently erected on the fifth earl's leases and to his building standards, with two exceptions: the old market house, conspicuous by its diamond-shaped clock, was not demolished until 1802; and on the other side of the street, the horseman is entering the Donegall Arms, which was knocked down in May of the year in which Nixon depicted it, to be replaced by a new building.

THE SOCIAL AND POLITICAL CLIMATE

The town in which the fifth earl had wrought improvement was well on the way to regarding his family as an irrelevance. The Chichester dispensation under which since 1613 Belfast had been incorporated as a borough, with a modicum of local self-government and the right to return two members to parliament, had become a self-perpetuating oligarchy. As the town developed, attracted trade and generated a breed of merchants and professional men well able to contribute ability and energy to the running of the town, it was a source of growing irritation that neither the Donegall family nor the government showed any signs of recognising the opportunities. The mercantile progress of Belfast took place in spite of, not because of, the dispensation. In composition, the population had undergone a change. The English settlers, anglicans by religious denomination, were joined in increasing numbers by presbyterians from the lowlands of Scotland, who by 1784 formed more than half of the rising mercantile and professional middle class. Roman Catholics, as yet a tiny minority, were not alone in feeling the effect of the legislation which became known as the penal code. Its object being to arrest the growth of popery, it did this by strengthening the established church, to the extent that all office holders under the crown had to take the sacrament in the Church of Ireland, a provision which bore as hard on non-anglican protestants as on Roman Catholics.

The townspeople of Belfast had perforce developed a capacity for fending for themselves. An example out of many, and one which was coming to a head when Bunting arrived in Belfast, concerned the vital ship-borne aspect of the town's commerce. The river Lagan dried out to two feet at low water at the Belfast quays and meandered through sandbanks and mudflats for three miles before deep water was reached at the pool of Garmoyle. The landing of cargo was an extremely difficult, slow and expensive business. The Chamber of Commerce petitioned the Irish parliament in 1785 for £2,000 towards the cost of cutting a straight channel. Parliament did not provide the money; but it transferred responsibility for control of the harbour from the apathetic corporation to a new Ballast Board, formed from the merchant community who had a direct interest in its efficient management and development.[5] The townspeople had also developed, not least through strong and continuing links with the Enlightenment Scotland of that day, an intellectual curiosity which extended into politics as well as other things. Effectively deprived of a say in the government of their town, but situated a long distance from their political masters in both London and Dublin, the people of Belfast were free to make up their own minds, to turn their energies into trade and commerce, and in the exercise of their intellectual curiosity, into philosophy, religion and politics. They backed parliamentary reform in Ireland and Catholic emancipation. Many Ulster presbyterians had emigrated across the Atlantic, and when the American colonies rose in rebellion Belfast's sympathy was with them. Troops were withdrawn from Ireland to fight in America. The townspeople had formed a company of the Volunteers, with weapons, uniforms and military band, six years before Edward Bunting came to Belfast.

MUSIC IN ST ANNE'S

Although the Belfast which Edward Bunting entered in 1784 to commence his apprenticeship had a larger population than Armagh, its musical status was not comparable. Armagh was a cathedral city, with an appropriate and long-established musical organisation. The anglican contribution to the musical life of Belfast in the eighteenth century was that of a parish church. An anglican church had been in existence at the foot of High Street, where the river Farset joins the Lagan, since the seventeenth century and possibly earlier. It was referred to as the old corporation church; it had been required practice for the sovereign to attend worship in procession, preceded by the mace and followed by the twelve burgesses and the free commoners. In the years of neglect the usage had lapsed and the fabric had deteriorated, and in 1777, being in Benn's words 'both unsafe and inconvenient', it was pulled down.[6] No mention has been found of an organ or of an organist. It was no doubt the intention of the fifth earl of Donegall, in an age when the great landed proprietors of Ulster

St Anne's parish church, opened in Donegall Street in 1776
from Benn's *History of the Town of Belfast*, 1823

vied with each other in lavish provision, that St Anne's, his new parish church in Donegall Street, should make a prestigious contribution to the ecclesiastical life of the town with its imposing façade and tower[7], and that the organ, said to have been commissioned from John Snetzler, should enhance its music appropriately.

A tendency in late sources to see the eighteenth-century parish church of a small town through the eyes of the later cathedral city has led to grandiose statements, such as that cathedral services were *fully instituted* in St Anne's as a new parish church, that it *continually* favoured high-class music and *often* had oratorios (italics added).[8] Such claims could be left aside, were it not that, if true, they would show an awareness of a corpus of church music that one would not expect in that church in the town of that time, with obvious implications for the positive growth of the musical life of the town at large. Little remains of the church's own records of its existence in the eighteenth century. Suffice it to say that at the present state of contemporary evidence available these claims are not substantiated. It is true that St Anne's had choristers. A choir of boys received £30 in salaries and a Mr Jones was paid £8 13s. for instructing them;[9] another contemporary source says that £5 13s. 9d. was provided for surplices.[10] A choir, however, was needed to sing the normal music of a parish church.[11] Nor is the presence of anthems in the sources to be taken as evidence of high capability in complex music. The eighteenth century was not a great period in the music of the anglican church at large; the spirit of reason and the Enlightenment were not conducive to worship in general, and were particularly opposed to liturgical forms.[12] The typical anthem in Michael Thomson's published collection of 1786 is for solo voice; sometimes there is a

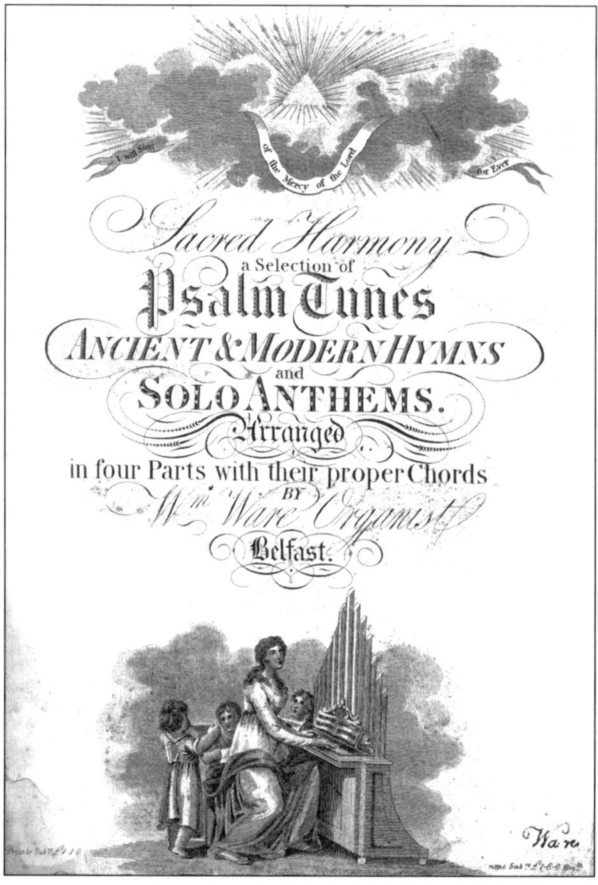

William Ware's *Sacred Harmony*, published in Dublin 1809, the frontispiece of the copy held in the Linen Hall Library.

duet section; the chorus sings short 'Hallelujahs' at the end followed by the 'Amen'; chorus entries in the body of the anthem are few and brief. The effect of the anthems depends principally upon the quality of the solo singers and of the organist. In Ware's book, Kent's 'Hear my prayer' is a verse anthem for two boys' voices; it has two contrasted duets, with the chorus joining in at the end; between them there is a treble aria and a short recitative.

Willliam Ware has left an indication of what the music was like in eighteenth-century St Anne's in his *Sacred Harmony*.[13] Despite his claim that the volume is for domestic use, one suspects that the music has not undergone much editing. The great majority of the sixty-odd pieces are tunes for the singing of metrical psalms, of which the words are given. The handful of hymns includes Charles Wesley's 'Lo, he comes with clouds descending', set to a version of 'Helmsley',[14] and 'The Portuguese Hymn on the Nativity' (set to words beginning 'All glorious God', familiar now as 'O come all ye faithful').[15] Less than a third have their composers named, and Handel is credited with eight. The few anthems included are short, with the exception of James Kent's 'Hear my prayer'. Evidence of 'high class' or oratorio music, as the late sources understood it, must be sought elsewhere. Most of the tunes are set out in four staves, for tenor, counter tenor and accompaniment. In some, bass voice is also called for, and there are choral passages in others in four parts, treble, counter, tenor and bass.

As early as 1716 in England Dr Thomas Bisse had declared that parish churches should conform as much as possible to the customs of the cathedral churches.[16] The degree of acceptance in Ireland of Bisse's dictum is not known. The presence of surplices in St Anne's may indicate an aspiration on the part of Ware or his vicar; or, perhaps more likely, it may have been the simplest way of ensuring that the boys appeared in church suitably clad.[17] For special occasions the choir no doubt sang special music. On the contemporary evidence available, however, the St Anne's choir of the eighteenth century sang 'cathedral service' only on two occasions, one of them with augmentation from outside. On Sunday 24 June 1781 there was masonic service and charity sermon 'for a cathedral service' in support of the opening of the new organ.[18] On Sunday 1 September 1799 there was a charity sermon, with cathedral service performed by the St Anne's forces augmented by visiting professional singer and instrumentalists.[19]

Three other special services may be noted. In the June of 1783, 1784 and 1785 masonic services were held, in which there were charity sermons, at which Michael Thomson of Hillsborough played the organ, and his choir sang hymns and anthems of his composition.[20] The performance of anthems and the presence of Thomson's choir do not *per se* make the services cathedral service in category (St Malachi's, Hillsborough was a parish church, like St Anne's). The three Michael Thomson days were all weekdays, and that, and perhaps their masonic character, may explain why, after the appointment of William Ware to St Anne's, the older organist was brought in with his choir from Hillsborough in three successive years; one of these services indeed, possibly two, took place after Bunting had become Ware's apprentice.

Whatever the state of congregational singing, there was no lack of interest in psalmody and hymnody, pursued outside, or alongside, the churches and certainly as a domestic activity. It is shown by the advertisements of freelance teachers such as Wilfred Richardson, opening a school at the old market house in April 1769 for teaching vocal music, 'particularly psalmody',[21] and John McVitty, using the market house as one of his schools of church music in 1787: Belfast would have his services on Wednesdays and Thursdays, Lisburn and Carrickfergus on two other days of the week each.[22] Richardson assured his readers that he would also 'wait upon ladies and gentlemen at their houses if desired'. Ware's book was aimed at church attenders, and also at private families who possessed 'the advantage of an Harpsichord or Piano Forte'. Some at least of the collections advertised by Magee the printer and publisher in 1775 look as if they were for home use: *Universal Psalmodist, Harmony Divine, Psalmody in Miniature*, Williams's *Christmas Anthems*, Jones's *Psalms, Divine Recreation*, Lady Glenarter's *Hymns*, Combes' *Psalms*, Arnold's *Compleat Psalmodist, Sunday's Amusement, Melodia Sacra, Magdalen Hymns and Anthems*, &c, &c.[23]

NOTES

1 In 1770 it had been 1,948, according to a census taken on behalf of the archbishop: LESLIE CLARKSON, 'Armagh 1770: portrait of an urban community', in DAVID HARKNESS and MARY O'DOWD (eds), *The town in Ireland* (Belfast, Appletree Press, 1981), p. 82.

2 Quoted in JONATHAN BARDON, *Belfast: an illustrated history* (Belfast, Blackstaff Press, 1982), p. 29.

3 C.E.B. BRETT, *Buildings of Belfast* (revised edition, Belfast, Friar's Bush Press, 1985), pp. 2–3.

4 BRETT, *Buildings of Belfast*, p. 4.

5 ROBIN SWEETNAM, 'The development of the port', in J.C. BECKETT *et al*, *Belfast: the making of the city 1800–1914* (Belfast, Appletree Press, 1983), pp. 57–58.

6 GEORGE BENN, *The history of the town of Belfast* (Belfast, Mackay 1823), pp. 112–113.

7 The illustration is from BENN, *Belfast*, 1823, facing p. 113. The Lawrence photograph in BRIAN M. WALKER and HUGH DIXON, *Belfast town 1864–1880* (Belfast, Friar's Bush Press, 1984), p. 34, more frequently encountered, shows the pediment raised in a later alteration and the clock re-located across the belfry opening, a view which Bunting would not have recognised.

8 H.M. THOMPSON and F.J. BIGGER, *The Cathedral Church of Belfast* (Belfast, Baird, 1925), pp. 7–9.

9 'BELFASTIENSIS' (ISAAC WARD), 'Old Belfast: William Ware, the first organist of the Parish Church, Belfast', *Belfast Evening Telegraph*, 6 October 1898. Ward had access to Ware's cashbook.

10 *The Journal of Disbursements of the Earl of Donegall's Antrim estate from July 1786 to October 1796*, reprinted in R.M. YOUNG, *Historical notices of old Belfast* (Belfast, Marcus Ward, 1896), p. 333.

11 The usage was not confined to the established church. In First Presbyterian church the singing was done, or at least led, by the singing clerk and his small group of singing boys; a singing clerk is recorded as 'before 1715' and another as 'before 1760': ALEXANDER GORDON, *Historic memorials of the First Presbyterian Church of Belfast* (Belfast, Marcus Ward, 1887), p. 122.

12 HORTON DAVIES, *Worship and theology in England* (5 volumes, Princeton, Princeton University Press, 1961–75), vol. 3, p. 52.

13 WILLIAM WARE, *Sacred harmony: a selection of psalm tunes, ancient and modern hymns and solo anthems* (Dublin, Powers, 1809).

14 Not the version familiar in modern hymnbooks, attributed to the Welsh itinerant disciple of Methodism, Thomas Olivers; the origin of the tune is much discussed, and St Anne's seems to have sung one of the variants.

15 Another familiar hymn of much discussed origin, words and text, but known as the Portuguese Hymn from the fact that Samuel Webbe the Elder, whose version of the tune gained most credence, was organist at the chapel of the Portuguese Embassy in London. Both this hymn and 'Lo, he comes with

clouds descending' came into currency in Ware's lifetime. They may show the breadth of hymnody in St Anne's; or they may be opportunist inclusions of Ware's – the Roman Catholic population in Belfast was growing, and Methodism after a slow start was to have its first meeting house in Belfast in 1806.

16 NICHOLAS TEMPERLEY, *The music of the English parish church* (2 volumes, Cambridge, Cambridge University Press, 1979), vol. 1, p. 105.

17 As in First Presbyterian, there was a philanthropic dimension to the recruitment of the choir and 'singing boys'; they came from poor homes or the Poor House.

18 *Belfast News-Letter*, 26–29 June 1781.

19 *BN-L*, 30 August 1799. Two solos and three choruses from *Messiah* were sung, hardly sufficient to justify the claim that St Anne's often had oratorios.

20 *BN-L*, 3–6 June 1783, *Belfast Mercury*, 18 June 1784, 28 June 1785.

21 *BN-L*, 4 April 1769.

22 *BN-L*, 2–6 November 1787.

23 *BN-L*, 15–19 September 1775.

3

BUNTING'S MASTER

'WILLIAM WARE, who has been employed these two Years by many Families of the first Distinction in the County of Down, is now returned from Dublin, where he has been a considerable Time for his Improvement.

He begs Leave to present his most respectful Compliments to the Ladies and Gentlemen of Belfast, where he wishes to make his principal Residence, if he is so happy to meet with sufficient Encouragement, in teaching the Harpsichord, Spinnet, Piano Forte, and Guittar, in the most approved Taste and Methods now in Use. His Terms are: for the Harpsichord, a Guinea Entrance, and a Guinea the twelve Lessons; Guittar, Half a Guinea Entrance, and Half a Guinea the twelve Lessons. Any Commands left for him with Mr. Welsh, at Mr. Marshall's in High-street, shall be duly attended to. An elegant Guittar, by an eminent Maker in Dublin, to be disposed of –

N.B. He tunes Harpsichords, and teaches in the Country as formerly.'

Belfast News-Letter, 28 June–2 July 1776

IN THE SCENARIO OF ARISTOCRATIC COMPETITION and emulation in which St Anne's was brought into being, its first organist, William Ware, seems out of scale.

Two neighbouring grandees, John O'Neill (later viscount) of Shane's Castle and the earl of Hillsborough (later marquis of Downshire), had appointed well-qualified and experienced Englishmen to look after the music of their parish churches. Ware was an Ulsterman, trained in Armagh cathedral. A late source[1] says he was trained under Robert Barnes. He was twenty years of age when he came to live in Belfast in 1776. It is suggested in the same source that he was appointed to St Anne's in that year, and that he had to do with the ordering and installation of the organ. There is room for doubt, especially in view of his age and his limited experience. Ware was not described as 'organist' in an advertisement until 1780,[2] nor as organist of St Anne's church until September 1781, when the opening of the organ was taking place.[3] In the advertisement, placed at the head of this chapter, in which he had introduced himself to the town four years earlier, setting out every attribute and qualification with which he would hope to gather a living in a strange town, including an ability to teach keyboard instruments, he had made no mention of St Anne's or an appointment as organist or choirmaster. It is not impossible that Ware, young as he was, may indeed have been prime mover from 1776; but it is also possible that he was a later appointment to the St Anne's post, possibly not the first choice.

William Ware,
first organist of St Anne's
ULSTER MUSEUM

Whatever the circumstances of his appointment, and whatever abilities he possessed as organ executant and teacher, William Ware found himself in an environment conducive to the exercise of additional talents. His career may be compared with those of the two other organists who have been mentioned. John O'Neill of Shane's Castle and his wife Henrietta were notable patrons of the arts. They built a private theatre on their estate at Edenduffcarrick, and John O'Neill established a private band;[4] it played for social occasions at Shane's Castle (including plays in the theatre and the visit of Mrs Siddons in 1785), for the riding of the franchises[5] and in a supporting capacity at elections. It is first heard of in Belfast in 1779 playing at a charity ball in the new Exchange Rooms,[6] and it played at several Belfast concerts. The post of organist of his parish church in Randalstown was in the gift of John O'Neill. His appointee, John Sharp, took pupils in keyboard and strings,[7] played the double bass in a concert in Belfast,[8] and described himself as professor of music and organist to O'Neill,[9] giving Shane's Castle as his address. He had been presumably appointed in the dual capacity of organist of the church and tutor of the band. By the end of the century, his artistic interests undimmed, John O'Neill had become a viscount and a prominent politician in the Irish parliament. He was fatally wounded in the insurgent attack on Antrim in June 1798,[10] and the influence of Shane's Castle on music in Belfast was dissipated. Nothing is heard again of the band: on John Sharp's death in 1803, if not before, it may have ceased to exist.

Wills Hill, second earl of Hillsborough, became prominent in politics in the reign of George III as secretary of state for the colonies. He built a parish church in Hillsborough, installed in it a Snetzler organ and appointed an organist from London, Michael Thomson. Having appointed him, he looked after him. The sovereignship of the corporation of Hillsborough was in the earl's gift, as was the deputy sovereignship and clerkship of the markets, all offices to which successively he appointed Michael Thomson. Thomson's own energy and ability enabled him to compose a good deal of church music and to have Trinity College, Dublin confer on him a doctorate in music; but the earl may have had a hand in his appointment to His Majesty's Band of Musicians in Ordinary.[11] The clearest example of his patron's beneficence is to be seen in the publication of a group of Michael Thomson's anthems.[12] Dedicated to the earl, it contains a list of no less than 367 subscribers. Most are Irish or Irish-domiciled, but the list also includes the organist of Westminster Abbey, the archbishops of both Canterbury and York, and many of the English aristocracy and government. The prime minister, Pitt, is down for two copies. The earl, backing his man to the hilt, has subscribed for fifty.

In contrast, the early musical life of Belfast developed without the direct participation and encouragement of its ruling family. William Ware, however, was a man to benefit from absentee patronage. John Sharp and Michael Thomson were well looked after by their respective patrons, but their capacity for independent action was circumscribed by the presence and wishes of their patrons. Ware operated under no such constraints. The absence of the fifth earl of Donegall left him free to exploit his own commercial talent. A hint of it appears in his arrival advertisement – 'an elegant Guitar, by an eminent Maker in Dublin, to be disposed of.' By the time he took Bunting into apprenticeship he had advertised a harpsichord for sale,[13] and the raffle at the Donegall Arms of a spinnet[14] and of a barrel organ.[15] His wife opened a boarding school for young ladies in their house in Donegall Street. English, French, drawing, dancing, writing and needlework were taught, and

> as Mr Ware teaches music, young ladies cannot fail making a greater proficiency in that accomplishment than in the generality of schools, as having the Master constantly in the house will be equal to private tuition.[16]

By 1785 he was advertising the sale of a piano forte, the instrument which was supplanting the harpsichord.[17] His advertisement of a harpsichord in 1789 is noteworthy on two counts. No doubt because the instrument was obsolescent, Ware went into detail:

> a fine-toned secondhand harpsichord, to be sold in compleat order, made by Shudi and Broadwood, London. It consists of a patent swell, 2 unisons, octave and harp stops and will be a great bargain.[18]

Also, the advertisement was placed, with an 'N.B.', at the foot of his wife's advertisement for the autumn re-opening of her school, an opportunity to sell keyboard instruments of which Ware availed himself regularly thereafter, avoiding the need for separate advertisement of his instruments for sale. The degree of freedom to develop his own business abilities in the absence of a resident patron is shown by the assertion that in some years the gross annual income of William Ware and his wife amounted to some £700–£800, at a time when his annual salary as organist of St Anne's was £50.[19] He was selective in his exploitation of the music market: apart from the guitar in his arrival advertisement he confined himself to keyboard instruments; there may have been something of a chamber organ market in private houses, but he seems not to have entered it. His wife's school gave him the ideal teaching situation: living at home, a steady supply of pupils, their fees collected within the school organisation, no need for him to waste a great deal of time travelling the countryside, as most music teachers (including his apprentice) were obliged to do.[20] In a community increasingly at odds with government, Ware confined his participation in political activity to foundation membership of the Belfast company of the Volunteers, where he played in the band.[21]

In 1784 Edward Bunting entered a town in which almost every avenue of activity was new with its way to make, or if established, was having to accommodate tradition to the urgent needs of urban growth and change. In the larger world there were upheavals soon to happen, and one, the revolt of the American colonies, had already taken place. It was a buoyant and stimulating place to complete his education and make his living. Of his progress under Ware as an organ pupil no contemporary accounts, much less appraisals, have survived. For his other musical activities Petrie provides both an account and a character:

> While thus engaged he had, in addition to his duties as assistant or sub-organist at the church, to act also as deputy teacher to Mr Weir's pupils on the piano-forte, throughout the neighbouring country; and the zeal of the young master to fulfil his duties were often productive of the most ludicrous results: for his young lady pupils, who were often many years older than himself, were accustomed to take his reproofs with anything but angelic temper, and we have heard him tell how a Miss Stewart, of Welmot, in the County of Down, was so astonished at his audacity that she indignantly turned round upon him and well boxed his ears. After a few years spent in this manner, he became a professor on his own account; and as his abilities as a performer had become developed, his company was courted by the higher class of the Belfast citizens, as well as by the gentry of the neighbourhood, and, in short, the boy prodigy became an idol amongst them. But, need we say that this was a most perilous position for a young man, subject to no control, imperfectly educated, with social temperament, and high animal spirits; obtaining, with ease, sufficient means to supply his wants, and without any higher objects of ambition to gratify than that which he had already

> compassed. Or should we wonder that, courted and caressed, flattered and humoured, as he was, he should have paid the usual penalty for such pampering – that his temper should have become pettish, and his habits wayward and idle – doing everything as he liked, with a reckless disregard of what might be thought of it. ... Wayward and pettish he remained through life, and for a long period – at least occasionally – idle, and, we fear, dissipated; for hard-drinking was the habit of the Belfastians in those days.[22]

It is not surprising to hear that the young apprentice was required to take the extramural teaching off his employer's hands. There is little likelihood that he would have been admitted to the cosy and lucrative music-teaching regime which Ware had established in his wife's school. That he should have had his ears boxed is for Petrie a sign of his character. It is also a social comment; the status of a professional musician was not far above that of a servant. Music was a desirable accomplishment – for men the violin and flute, for women the piano and guitar – but within social limits. In the late eighteenth century Lord Chesterfield's famous advice to his son was in circulation in Belfast, somewhat paraphrased, in a conduct-and-courtesy book:

> Music is commonly reckoned one of the liberal arts, and undoubtedly is so; but to be piping or fiddling at a concert is degrading to a man of fashion. If you love music, hear it; pay fiddlers to play to you, but never fiddle yourself. It makes a gentleman appear frivolous and contemptible, leads him frequently into bad company, and wastes that time which might otherwise be well employed.[23]

As elsewhere, the advice was sufficiently ignored for a concert life to develop in which some gentlemen played, more became members of musical clubs, and more still, with their womenfolk, comprised the audiences which came to hear them, but the social gap between them and the professional musician remained. The earl of Mornington, father of the Duke of Wellington, who died in 1781,

> also earned immortality as the first member of the British aristocracy who dared to walk through the London streets openly and unashamedly carrying a violin case.[24]

Fox says that he 'became efficient, not only at tuning, but actually at repairing and constructing pianos'.[25] That Bunting should have been taught how keyboard instruments were made, and the skills of tuning and repairing, is no more than a pupil would expect of a master, especially the deeply expert Ware. Bunting did not live in his master's house as did many an apprentice, but lodged elsewhere in Donegall Street with the family of John McCracken, of whom the two children best known to later times are Mary Ann McCracken and Henry Joy McCracken. Such general education as he had – and it may have been considerable – he obtained from the McCrackens. As to the consequences, that 'imperfect of education' and 'pampered' because of his abilities as a performer, 'his temper should have become pettish and his habits wayward and idle', one suspects again that Petrie's authority is remembering his standing as pianist and performer-in-demand 'with advantages' while also depicting himself as a rogue. The portrait is rather at variance with that given by so acute a contemporary observer as Mrs Martha McTier. In the after-glow of the publication of the first collection, she calls him 'the famous musician':

> sugar plums and sweeties is his greatest temptation, for he despises both money and praise and is thought a good-hearted original.[26]

CONCERT LIFE

Shortly before Bunting joined him, Ware had begun to venture into yet another aspect of local music-making. The public concert, a relative newcomer to the music scene in the world at large,[27] is not heard of in Belfast until the mid-point of the century, when a party of professional musicians gave concerts in June 1750 in the old market house en route from Dublin to Edinburgh, and in September on their way back.[28] There is no evidence of help from, or participation by, local musicians. One of the party, the flautist Rocke, advertised on their departure, offering tuition in a variety of instruments and expressing an intention to stay in the area 'if encourag'd'.[29] Instances of isolated concerts begin to drift through the pages of the *Belfast News-Letter* in the 1750s and 1760s. There appears in 1768 the first evidence of the existence of the Belfast Musical Society:

> There will be a Concert at the Market-House on Tuesday evening next: to begin precisely at half past six – No Person whatever to be

> admitted without a ticket.[30]

A month later another advertisement appeared, apparently referring to a series:

> The Gentlemen's Monthly Concert begins at seven o'clock this evening. It is requested that, to prevent interruption in the Performance, the Audience will keep Silence.[31]

It is another month before the body is at last named:

> The Belfast Musical Society will have a publick Concert this evening. To begin precisely at half after six o'clock.[32]

It seems to have been a typical eighteenth-century gentlemen's club, its members meeting regularly to play and eat supper, its constitution concerned to admit those who were socially congenial and to exclude those who were not. Since it was a private club whose members lived locally in what was still a small town, its advertisements were infrequent; on a strict need-to-know basis they carried a minimum of information, and none at all as to what was played and by whom, even in its 'public' concerts. The society is not heard of for longish periods.[33] Perhaps it went in and out of existence, beginning afresh each time; perhaps, and it seems more likely, it remained in unbroken existence and for long periods saw no need to make use of the public prints.[34] In 1768 it appointed as professional leader a Mr Rocke from Lisburn, who may have been the 1750 flautist. The arrangement lasted less than a season. A Mr Crowe and his wife, a well known singer in Dublin under her maiden name Rachel Baptist, performed in Belfast for the full season of 1772–3; he may have been the leader of the Musical Society, although the relationship is not clear. By this time the society was running regular series of subscription concerts. It seems to have had nearly a monopoly of the concert life of the town. Only a handful of other concerts took place in the 1760s and 1770s. That held in the Poor House in March 1778 is unique in advertising its full programme, with some composers named; no performers are named, however.[35] The Musical Society broke with custom by advertising one of its concerts in the following year in similar detail.[36]

As other public concerts begin to appear with more frequency, William Ware's interest becomes evident. It is possible that the band of the Musical Society had the stiffening of a few professionals.[37] During a theatre season there would have been a professional theatre band; since the theatre usually gave three performances a week, its players may have been available for concerts on their free nights. Also, the band of the regiment in garrison was often available for public events. Evidence of locally-based professional musicians who were in neither category is hard to find but not impossible; there is mention of professionals in the town as early as the 1720s.[38] The presence of a concerto in a concert programme is an indicator of the presence of a soloist, either based in the town or a visitor. The Poor House concert of 1778 had no less than three concertos. A concert in March 1780 in the new Exchange Rooms has its programme advertised, and it contains two harpsichord concertos.[39] A visiting soloist on either occasion would expect to have been named, and the only local keyboard professional who is heard of up to this time is William Ware. A further hint of Ware's involvement in the latter concert is the presence in the advertisement of 'gentlemen of Armagh choir'; Ware kept his links with the cathedral. In a charity concert of January 1782, Ware appears by name; the concert is 'to be conducted by Messrs Ware, Byrne and Atkins'.[40] Michael Atkins was the manager of the Belfast theatre, and Byrne was his company musician and leader of the band. No other names are given. Atkins was a musically versatile man of the theatre,[41] and with Ware's harpsichord and Byrne's violin the three professionals may well have performed the entire concert, and for that matter, provided the music for the customary ball afterwards. In 1784 there were two notable concerts. In a charity concert in May Ware is advertised as the conductor and Byrne is to lead the band.[42] No other performers' names are given, but nearly every instrumental piece has its composer's name; the forces need not have been large, but they were competent to play overtures by Abel and Haydn,[43] a harpsichord concerto (was Ware the soloist?) and two Haydn string quartets. There was a substantial vocal content of songs, duets, a glee and a chorus by Handel (the only vocal composer named).

Edward Bunting may have arrived in Belfast in time for that concert; he could certainly have been there for the second concert in December, the first to have visiting celebrities. Unusually, it received a puff in advance of the advertisement:

> A few days ago arrived in town from Shanescastle ... Mr and Master Weichsel, justly celebrated in the musical world, particularly the latter, who, though not yet 17 years of age, is esteemed the greatest performer on the Violin in Europe, having led the best bands in London and Dublin for some years past. We hear he will shortly perform in a Concert to be held at our New Assembly Rooms ...[44]

and equally unusually, a report:

> a very brilliant assemblage of Ladies and Gentlemen honoured Messrs Weichsell at the Concert last night in the New Assembly Rooms, and were unanimous in applauding the merits of the several capital Musicians who performed ... The Right Hon. John O'Neill, and his Lady, were present at the Concert last night.[45]

John O'Neill's private band had played at a ball in Belfast five years earlier,[46] but this was its first appearance at a concert. In the grand march at the end it was joined by the band of the garrison regiment. The advertised programme included a symphony by Stamitz and a quartet by Haydn. The Weichsells, father and son, were named, the singer Urbani and the cellist Dell' Oca. Of the local professionals Ware was named as the harpsichord soloist, Byrne and Erskine of the theatre band as taking part in a quintet (composer unnamed) with the Weichsells and Dell' Oca. In personnel, quality of music and performance it was the stuff of the Rotunda concerts in Dublin from which the visitors had come. Young Bunting was unlikely to have heard the like in Armagh or Drogheda. Whether or not John O'Neill was a member of the Belfast Musical Society (he could have been) the concert was not under that body's auspices. The high price of the seats (5s. 5d. against the society's 2s. 2d.) did not apparently prevent a full house, and there were no restrictions on admission.

A year later, the O'Neills entertained a further group of notable musicians, and Belfast was again to benefit by a concert in the Exchange Rooms, the performers including O'Neill's band.[47] The visiting soloists were described as Messrs Mahoon, O'Kelly and Ashe. 'Mr Mahoon' was John Mahon, violinist and pioneer clarinettist, the most notable of a family of English musicians of Irish origin. Andrew Ashe was in his late twenties, some ten years younger than Mahon, and came from Lisburn; he had yet to make his considerable London and European reputation as a flautist. Ashe played flute concertos,

Mahon a violin concerto and also one for clarinet; there was a concerto for two violins (Mahon and O'Kelly), a concertante for O'Kelly (viola), Mahon (clarinet) and Ashe. In default of composers' names, it seems likely that the composers of the music of all the concertos and the concertante were Mahon and Ashe. There were symphonies by Haydn and Dittersdorf, and to end with, a grand march 'composed for the occasion'. The two concerts under the O'Neills' patronage had put on display the taste in music and the playing standards of the London concerts of the day, via those of Dublin, and they had been succcessful. A substantial concert audience was available in Belfast, to the promoter or promoting body which could attract it. It was William Ware who saw and was prepared to exploit the opportunity to put the subscription concert on a commercial basis in Belfast, in line with practice in more developed concert life elsewhere.

Ware had played a harpsichord solo in the Weichsells' concert, but his name does not appear in the programme of the Ashe and Mahon concert. Mrs Ware was in bad health. In May of that year she had to advertise that she was 'obliged to resign the school' on 1 July, and that the school would be opened by the assistant, Miss Agnew, who had 'taken a house for the purpose in Donegall Street two doors above Mrs Ware's'.[48] Mrs Ware died on 18 September.[49] A venture into the new territory of concert promotion was out of the question in the 1786–7 season. But at the beginning of the 1787–8 season Ware placed a comprehensive advertisement:

> MR WARE,
>
> Most respectfully informs the Ladies and Gentlemen of Belfast and its Vicinity, that (in consequence of several applications made to him) he will have the ensuing winter, Thirteen grand Concerts of Vocal and Instrumental Musick; after each of which will be a Ball, with Tea, cards &c – which will commence the latter end October next, and continue regularly once a fortnight. The Concert will consist of three acts, in each of which will be a Vocal Performer, also a Select Piece for either the Violin or Grand Piano Forte, and from the promise of assistance from several Gentlemen Performers, he presumes the Instrumental Parts will be so regulated, as to give entire satisfaction to those who may favour him with their Support. It having been intimated by some Gentlemen, that the Concerts might injure the fund (arising from the Assemblies) to the Poor-House: Mr Ware will

> therefore give a night (gratis) to that Charity, which he hopes will fully obviate every objection.The Undertaking being New in Belfast, and attended with a heavy Expence, Subscriptions will be thankfully received on the following Conditions – For two Guineas a Ticket, to be admitted each Night; for five guineas, three Tickets, which will only be transferable in a Family. Non-Subscribers five Shillings British each. As a first rate Vocal Performer must be engaged during the season, Mr Ware requests an early return of the Names of such of his Friends as mean to subscribe. The Subscription to be paid when the tickets are delivered.[50]

It was the sort of pre-season advertisement on which Ware had no doubt consulted Ashe and Mahon and had then adapted to Belfast conditions. He had identified such audience preferences as the need for soloists and a nod to charity. The ambitious schedule of thirteen fortnightly concerts spanned a full season from October to April. The orchestra would consist of locally-based musicians. The several 'Gentlemen Performers' may have included members of the Belfast Musical Society; professionals were not referred to as 'gentlemen'. It is a reasonable assumption that Ware could also have called on occasion on members of the garrison band, the theatre band and perhaps John O'Neill's band. Each concert needed as soloists a singer, a violinist and a pianist. Ware could have seen himself, and perhaps his pupil Edward Bunting, in the role of occasional piano soloist. The choice of Thursday as concert night should have ensured a larger audience than an evening when the theatre was playing; it would also have freed Byrne to play in the concerts, as leader of the orchestra and occasional violin soloist. As it happened, Byrne's presence in the town for the whole of this season could be relied upon. Michael Atkins, his employer, was still manager of a circuit which included theatres in Newry and Londonderry, but his interest in Newry was by now nominal only,[51] and a few weeks before Ware's advertisement he had announced a new theatre for Londonderry, which was not to open until 1789.[52] The most important soloist was the singer, and there was no person of concert quality to be found in Belfast or its neighbourhood. It is unlikely in any case that Ware intended as a matter of course that all his concert forces should be locally based. He of all people would have realised that now that the Belfast audience had heard the Weichsells, Ashe and Mahon they would not subscribe to a series offering locally-based talent only.

Had Ware then already engaged a sufficient number of professional soloists to sustain his entire series, in such uncharted territory as Belfast? Who were they? If they had not yet been engaged, what had led Ware to believe that they could be? It seems unlike William Ware to have taken such a leap in the dark. The advertisement, for whatever reasons, was certainly premature; not one concert of the series took place. Had Ware received promises, perhaps through contacts like Mahon and Ashe, which were not kept? There is evidence that it was called off early: Byrne's Thursday nights were free when he placed an advertisement in the first week of September, acquainting 'the Musical Society of Larne and the inhabitants in general' that he would be able to visit them regularly once a month from the 23rd.[53]

In the 1787–8 season the only concert Ware was able to promote was an opportunist one which narrowly avoided failure, when he caught at short notice a celebrity on his way to London and

> prevailed upon Mr Fisher, doctor of music in the university of Oxford, to postpone his journey for a few days in order to gratify the public curiosity with the performance of so great a master.[54]

There were hurried arrangements; Ware had to take the Donegall Arms rather than the Exchange Rooms, and he presumed on the availability of the gentlemen choristers of Armagh.[55] They did not materialise, and it was John Abraham Fisher himself who rescued the event by agreeing to give a solo violin recital (a concert format very rare at this period). It is indicative of the primacy of the vocal content of a concert that Fisher and Ware reduced the admission prices from 5s. 5d. to 3s. 3d.[56]

There are no advertisements of concerts promoted by Ware or by anyone else in the following season. It would be some time before roads and transport would be good enough for an artist to travel from Dublin to Belfast and back for a single concert. A promoter, it seemed, had to rely on the rare chance of an artist travelling, like Fisher, between Ireland and Britain, or on the presence nearby of a group of artists on a visit to a big house. The latter circumstance occurred in the 1789–1790 season. A group of concerts began with a 'Harmonic Fete' advertised for Thursday 22 October in the Exchange

Rooms with Mrs Arnold, who described herself as 'first singer of the Rotunda'.[57] Tickets were to be had at the Donegall Arms, the Exchange Coffee House and from Mrs Arnold herself; it was obviously her own promotion. She advertised a second concert for Friday 30 'by desire of the people who could not attend her first', and promised half the receipts to the Charitable Society.[58] The same issue of the *Belfast News-Letter* contained notice of a concert at Antrim on the same evening, at which Mahon was to be first violin and Ashe principal flute. Tickets were to be had from Ashe and Mahon at Shane's Castle; they were obviously guests again of the O'Neills. A week later Mrs Arnold was to sing at a concert and ball at Hillsborough;[59] she was enjoying, it would seem, the hospitality of the family whose head had now become the marquis of Downshire. It was Ware who brought the talents together, announcing his first concert for Thursday 19 November, having engaged Mahon, Ashe and Mrs Arnold.[60] Concerts would continue every Thursday for eight performances, the week of Christmas excepted. There would be a ball each night, and the band would be led by Mahon. Mrs Arnold would sing twice in each concert and in each there would be solo concertos by Mahon and Ashe.

Ware had moved quickly to secure his soloists, but the first concert did not take place until 30 November (a Monday),[61] after changes of day of the week and difficulty in hiring the Exchange Rooms. To the efforts of his master to establish systematic promotion of public concerts young Edward Bunting was more than an interested bystander. The second concert, on Monday 7 December,[62] was noteworthy for his own concert debut, at the age of sixteen, as a keyboard soloist, probably on the harpsichord, playing a popular showpiece of the day, Kocswara's 'The Battle of Prague'. He was in the best professional company of the day, playing the most fashionable music. Mrs Arnold's party piece from *The Duenna*, 'Adieu, thou dreary pile', had flute obbligato by Ashe. Ashe and Mahon played a concerto each. The concert began with an overture by Vanhall and the second half with a symphony by Haydn. There was a Pleyel flute quartet. The orchestra was enlarged by the band of John O'Neill. Bunting played a harpsichord concerto in the next Ware concert. It did not take place until 28 December and proved to be the last in the series.[63]

Not that the emergent concert public of Belfast were to be disappointed; they were to have a total of seven concerts, all involving these Rotunda artists. From mid-December the celebrities had begun to put on their own benefits, promoted by themselves, performing new crowd-pullers and the most popular items from what they had already performed. It was a custom well known in the theatre, as no doubt Ware had heard from Atkins; but he had not reckoned with sustaining the financial loss of a large part of the revenues of more than half his season. Of the eight concerts advertised by Ware as his series, only three had materialised. Ashe had his benefit on 16 December;[64] Mahon advertised his for 30 December, two days later than the Ware concert, no doubt damaging Ware's audience,[65] and Mrs Arnold held hers on 13 January.[66] If Ware had known in advance, no doubt he would have sewn up the arrangements more tightly. But whatever attempts he made to put on further concerts in his own series, none materialised, and after Ashe and Mahon had a final joint benefit on 3 February[67] they left for Dublin to perform at concerts in the Rotunda.[68] Ware had been no match for the three seasoned celebrities, who had milked the benefit system for what it was worth. Not for the only time in his life, Ware had been ahead of his time, but even when at last his professional soloists were to hand, he had discovered to his cost the difficulties of providing the subscribers to his series with visiting soloists who knew how to manipulate the market.

Edward Bunting, having made his own concert debut in exalted musical company, might have looked forward to a regular place in future concert series, had the times been tranquil. But by now they were not. The turbulence in which the eighteenth century was to end was well advanced, not only in Ireland; the 1789 concerts began in the immediate aftermath of the fall of the Bastille. In the final decade of the century concert activity in Belfast vanished almost totally from sight.

William Ware, recognising a failure of judgment in entering the field of concert promotion, found himself thrown back on those enterprises which he had pioneered with success. His main teaching activity had been interrupted following his wife's death. Advertisements for the school cease for some years, and when they reappear Ware has married a second wife, said by a late source to have been the Miss Agnew who was his first wife's assistant.[69] There are brief notices of 'Mrs Ware's school' in 1790, and then a substantial advertisement in 1791, giving subjects and fees in detail, proclaiming the return of full operation.[70] His other business interest, in the sale of keyboard instruments, had begun to increase significantly. When the piano boom set in,[71] attracting general merchants in the town to a growing market,[72] Ware, far from being left behind, was able to keep his nose in front. If he lacked the warehouse space to carry stock in variety, he had professional business contacts with Broadwood and other makers. He had offered also, since the days of his arrival advertisement, an expertise in tuning and servicing which set him ahead of his rivals.[73] Fully aware of the piano boom and the cessation of manufacture of harpsichords, he also knew that the harpsichord had by no means passed out of use, that there would be a secondhand market for some time, and that he was well placed to offer the necessary services of tuning, repair and, if desired, improvement. At the end of the advertisement restoring his wife's school, Ware added his customary postscript, this time to the effect that he had for sale 'a fine-toned secondhand harpsichord in compleat order, to which he added a Celestina stop, and will be sold one half under first cost'.[74] He had the better of both worlds, the old and the new. In the final decade of the century, he rarely offers a single instrument, and his advertisement is often for several harpsichords and several pianos.[75]

In 1794 he and his wife embarked on a new venture. Belfast was an increasingly disturbed place to live in, and if the Wares were attracted by a move out to the neighbouring countryside, they were doubtless not alone. In February they announced their intention to remove their school on 1 May from Donegall Street to their house at Sea View on the road to Carrickfergus. They promised 'subjects as before' and, up with the times as ever, 'bathing annexed now'.[76] By the end of their first school year on the new site, Ware was 'setting part or all of his farm there'.[77] The whole experiment was to be shortlived. The advertisement for the reopening in the following year included a ban on use of the bathing house 'upon any other terms than one guinea during the season',[78] and Mrs Ware shortly afterwards gave an early notice that 'finding a country residence exceedingly inconvenient in many respects', she intended moving to continue the school in a house in Arthur Street in town, 'lately occupied by General Nugent'.[79] By the following autumn term, the school was opening in its new location.[80]

NOTES

1 'BELFASTIENSIS', *BET*, 1898.
2 *BN-L*, 12–15 December 1780.
3 *BN-L*, 28 September–2 October 1781.
4 'It was a *sine qua non* in the engaging of a servant, that he should play upon an instrument': JOHN BERNARD, *Retrospections of the stage* (2 volumes, London, H. Colburn and R. Bentley, 1830), vol.1, p. 321. Bernard was an actor in Michael Atkins' company in Belfast in the early 1780s, and appears as a member of the Adelphi Club in the painting in the Linen Hall Library.
5 *Belfast Evening Post*, 10 July 1786.
6 *BN-L*, 29 January–2 February 1779.
7 *BN-L*, 12 September 1788.
8 *BN-L*, 18 December 1789.
9 *BN-L*, 10 January 1794.
10 For his death see Dr Halliday to Lord Charlemont in *The manuscripts and correspondence of James, first Earl of Charlemont 1745–99* (2 volumes, London, Historical Manuscripts Commission, 1891, 1894), vol. 2, pp. 328–30, and A.T.Q. STEWART, *The summer soldiers: the 1798 Rebellion in Antrim and Down* (Belfast, Blackstaff Press, 1995), pp. 111–112, 116, 117.
11 *BN-L*, 10–13 April 1787. For Burney's and Parke's annoyance at the need for influence at court to obtain places in this sinecure, see SIMON MCVEIGH, *The violinist in London's concert life 1750–84* (New York, Garland, 1989), p. 36.
12 *Six Anthems performed in Hillsborough Church: the music composed by Michael Thomson, Mus. D.* (Hillsborough, 1786). A copy is held in the Linen Hall Library.
13 *BN-L*, 12–15 December 1780.
14 *BN-L*, 27 February 1781.
15 *BM*, 24 October 1783.
16 *BN-L*, 19 September 1780.
17 *BM*, 14 January 1785.
18 *BN-L*, 28 August–1 September 1789.
19 'BELFASTIENSIS', *BET*, 1898. Ward, as already noted, had access to Ware's cashbook.
20 Richard Langdon, succeeding Langrishe Doyle as organist of Armagh Cathedral, advertised his willingness to teach 'at any distance within one day's journey of Armagh': *BN-L*, 24–27 July 1781.
21 'A Roll of the Belfast 1st Volunteer Company, date of their association the 17th of March 1778, published by order of the Company, March 31, 1781', reprinted in THOMSON and BIGGER, *Cathedral Church*: Appendix XVI shows Ware as 'in the band'. Isaac Ward found from Ware's cashbook that 'he joined the corps as a musician, and appears to have played the hautboy or oboe': 'BELFASTIENSIS', *BET*, 1898.
22 PETRIE, *Bunting*, p. 67.
23 *The young Gentleman and Ladies MONITOR, being a collection of select pieces*

from our modern writers: particularly calculated to form the mind and manners of the youth of both sexes, and adapted to the use of schools and academies, by Hamilton Moore, Esq. Used in the Academy, Belfast (Belfast, 1788), p. 284.

24 BERNARR RAINBOW, *The land without music* (London, Novello, 1967), p. 25.

25 FOX, *Annals*, p. 12.

26 Mrs McTier to William Drennan, undated, probably 1798, in JEAN AGNEW (ed.), *The Drennan-McTier Letters* (3 volumes, Dublin, The Women's History Project in association with Irish Manuscripts Commission, 1998–99), No 731, vol. 2, p. 373.

27 Those given in London by John Bannister in 1672 are said in many authorities to have been the first in England.

28 ROY JOHNSTON, 'The pleasures and penalties of networking: John Frederick Lampe in the summer of 1750', in SIMON MCVEIGH and SUSAN WOLLENBERG (eds), *Concert life in eighteenth-century Britain* (Aldershot, Ashgate, 2004).

29 *BN-L*, 2 September 1750.

30 *BN-L*, 20 May 1768.

31 *BN-L*, 21 June 1768.

32 *BN-L*, 19 July 1768.

33 Proof of the existence of the Belfast Musical Society rests almost solely on newspaper advertisements over a period of eighteen years from 1768 to 1786, for half of which time there are no advertisements at all. The periods for which there is positive evidence amount to one stretch of seven years and two of less than one year each. None of its concerts received report or review.

34 Several of the features of the Belfast Musical Society are discernible in the Anacreontic Society of the nineteenth century.

35 *BN-L*, 27 February–3 March 1778.

36 *BN-L*, 8–12 October 1779.

37 During the eighteenth century and much of the nineteenth, 'band' meant 'orchestra', and 'orchestra' meant the place in the auditorium where the band played.

38 The funeral register of First Presbyterian Church, which gives occupations as well as names and addresses, records at 29 March 1721 the funeral of a brother of 'Archelb Miler, ffidler, living in noarstreet [North Street]', and at 17 November 1726 that of a child of 'will McDowaille, ffidler'. The sexton who made the entries spelt phonetically: 'Samull McCalliue' had a child buried on 9 January 1732; it is when his occupation, 'museshanar', is pronounced aloud that it is realised that he was a 'musicianer'. I am grateful to Rev D.G. Banham and Mr Tom Moore of First Presbyterian church for allowing me to consult the original of this register.

39 *BN-L*, 10–14 March 1780.

40 *BN-L*, 22–25 January 1782.

41 John Bernard described him as 'a pretty singer but not a clever manager': *Retrospections*, vol. 1, p. 308.

42 *BN-L*, 30 April–4 May 1784.

43 In the eighteenth century the term 'overture' was often used for what would now be catalogued as a symphony.
44 *BM*, 16 November 1784.
45 *BM*, 10 December 1784.
46 *BN-L*, 29 January–2 February 1779.
47 *BM*, 13 January 1786.
48 *BN-L*, 12–16 May 1786.
49 *BN-L*, 19–22 September 1786.
50 *BN-L*, 10–14 August 1787.
51 WILLIAM SMITH CLARK, *The Irish stage in the county towns 1720 to 1800* (Oxford, Clarendon Press, 1963), pp. 195–96.
52 SMITH CLARK, pp. 206–7.
53 *BN-L*, 4–7 September 1787.
54 *BN-L*, 29 January–1 February 1788.
55 *BN-L*, 1–5 February 1788.
56 *BN-L*, 5–8 February 1788.
57 *BN-L*, 13–16 October 1789.
58 *BN-L*, 23–27 October 1789.
59 *BN-L*, 30 October–3 November 1789.
60 *BN-L*, 30 October–3 November 1789.
61 Brief report in *BN-L*, 1–4 December 1789.
62 *BN-L*, 1–4 December 1789.
63 *BN-L*, 8–11 December 1789.
64 *BN-L*, 8–11 December 1789.
65 *BN-L*, 15–18 December 1789.
66 *BN-L*, 29 December 1789–1 January 1790.
67 *BN-L*, 22–26 January 1790.
68 The only extant programme of a Rotunda concert of 1790, that of 27 April, the last of a series of six, shows the band under the direction of Ashe, with Mahon leading: BRIAN BOYDELL, *Rotunda music in eighteenth-century Dublin* (Dublin, Irish Academic Press, 1992), p. 169n.
69 'BELFASTIENSIS', *BET*, 1898.
70 *BN-L*, 28 January–1 February 1791.
71 After 1770 the period of gestation was over and the piano forte entered a phase of rapid technical and commercial advance: CYRIL EHRLICH, *The piano: a history* (revised edition, Oxford, Clarendon Press, 1990), p. 14. Broadwood was to stop making harpsichords for a dying market in 1793: ibid., p.18.
72 James Magee, who had included musical instruments in his multifarious wares, was the first to enter the market, offering pianos (but not tuning and repair): *BN-L*, 16–20 January, 21–25 August 1789.
73 That it was an essential element of piano supply was something which the merchants took some time to learn, even after it had become a specialised market. It was well into the nineteenth century, after Ware had died, that they began to advertise the presence in their premises of qualified tuners, often from an English factory. The story of Joseph Hart touches the present essay at

several points. As a professional musician, he succeeded Edward Bunting as organist of St George's, and as a businessman he concentrated on pianos, tuning them himself. In 1858 he announced the employment of a tuner from Collard and Collard called William Grant Churchill: *BN-L*, 18 September 1858. His son, Edward Bunting Hart, took Churchill into partnership, and the firm of Hart and Churchill remained in business in Belfast until recent years.

74 *BN-L*, 25–28 January 1791.

75 For example: 'Two secondhand harpsichords, and two new piano fortes, to be disposed of': *BN-L*, 21–25 January 1792. The breadth of his service is shown in: 'Mr Ware, selling a new Southwell piano forte, solicits orders for musical instruments and can supply them at short notice from London and Dublin on more reasonable terms than formerly; all instruments chosen by him are kept in tune (in town *gratis*) for 12 months': *BN-L*, 9 December 1800.

76 *BN-L*, 21–25 February 1794.

77 *BN-L*, 27–31 July 1795.

78 *BN-L*, 25–29 July 1796.

79 *BN-L*, 7–10 October 1796.

80 *BN-L*, 24 July 1797.

4
THE HARPERS

'Ten harpers only responded to this call, a sufficient proof of the declining state of the art, and of the necessity which now manifestly existed of noting down as many as possible of those musical treasures which might so soon perish along with their venerable repositories. This was the office assigned to the Editor, and in discharging it, he first imbibed that passion for Irish melody which has never ceased to animate him since.'

(BUNTING 1840, preface, p. 63)

FOR WARE, ONE OF THE INCONVENIENCES of country residence must have been the journey to St Anne's to discharge his duties as organist. It was the more onerous because of the frequent absence of his assistant organist. The story of the meeting of the harpers in 1792 has been often told, and need only be briefly and selectively summarised. The earliest mention of music in the *Belfast News-Letter* is of the harp, albeit in a non-musical context:

> Yesterday a strolling person … was seen in this place … having left a harp at the Widow McCommons at the Long Bridge near Belfast, where said harp still remains. It has carved on it these words: 'This harp was made for Sir Henry Piercy in the year 1722'.[1]

Bunting in his final collection was to include a chapter which he called 'Anecdotes of the more distinguished harpers of the last two centuries'.[2] Acknowledging Arthur O'Neill and Denis Hempson as sources, he commences with Rory Dall O'Cahan, as well known in seventeenth-century Scotland as in Ireland and described by Sir Walter Scott in *The Legend of Montrose* as 'the most famous harper of the Western Highlands', and continues by way of Cornelius Lyons, harper to the earl of Antrim, and others, to Carolan, of whom, he says:

> so much has been written, that comparatively little remains to be done here, either in illustrating the fertility of his genius, or in recounting the whimsical adventures and practical jokes for which his memory is famous.

Carolan died thirty-five years before Bunting was born; the link with the harpers who played at Belfast in 1792 was provided by Denis Hempson, who was born in 1695. A younger contemporary of Hempson, who was born in 1715 but died before the festival, was Dominic Mungan, whose 'exquisite taste and finger' were recalled by the editor of the *Belfast News-Letter* in his reports of the festival. He appears – the first reference to the harp being played in Belfast – in 1762:

> Dominick the Harper returns his hearty thanks to the Gentlemen and Ladies who have been so kind as to favour him with their company, and begs leave to inform them, that he intends to perform at Tim's Coffee House next Monday evening, being the last time of his performance here, at half an hour after six. Price of admittance 1s. 1d. as usual.[3]

By the second half of the eighteenth century the ranks of the harpers, once the resident minstrels of the native aristocracy, had thinned almost to disappearance, notwithstanding their adoption by the new aristocracy. Attempts at rescue had been made, notably at Granard in County Longford in the 1780s; competitions had been held in three successive years and prizes awarded. In December 1791 a handbill was circulated in Belfast 'and the neighbourhood' with the object of raising money by subscription for a further meeting:[4]

> SOME Inhabitants of BELFAST, feeling themselves interested in every thing which relates to the Honor, as well as the Prosperity of their Country; propose to open a Subscription, which they intend to apply in attempting to revive and perpetuate – *The Ancient Music and Poetry of Ireland.* They are solicitous to preserve from oblivion, the few fragments which have been *permitted* to remain as Monuments of the refined Taste and Genius of their Ancestors.
>
> In order to carry this Project into execution, it must appear obvious to those acquainted with the situation of this Country, that it will be necessary to assemble the HARPERS, those descendants of our antient Bards, who are at present, almost exclusively posessed of all that remains of the *Music, Poetry*, and *Oral Traditions* of IRELAND.
>
> It is proposed, that the Harpers should be induced to assemble at BELFAST, (suppose on the 1st of *July* next,) by the distribution of such Prizes as may seem adequate to the Subscribers: And that a Person well versed in the Language and Antiquities of this Nation, should attend, with a skilful Musician to transcribe and arrange the most beautiful and interesting parts of their Knowledge. An undertaking of this nature, will undoubtedly meet the approbation of Men of Refinement and Erudition in every Country: And when it is considered, how intimately the *Spirit* and *Character* of a PEOPLE are connected with their *National Poetry* and *Music*, it is presumed, that the IRISH PATRIOT and POLITICIAN will not deem it an object unworthy his patronage and protection.[5]

The handbill repays scrutiny. The intention to 'revive and perpetuate' is stated straightaway, and amplified later. The words 'and perpetuate' are omitted from the transcription in the *Belfast News-Letter* of 23–27 December; but probably nothing more need be read into that than the removal by the editor of what he saw as a tautology. In the second paragraph the drafters of the handbill assert confidently that the 'few remains' of the music are 'almost exclusively' in the hands of the 'aristocratic tradition' of the harpers. Bunting's decision to go in search of a much larger corpus transmitted by singer, fiddler and piper would show these to be misapprehensions. The first half of the third paragraph indicates an intention to follow the path laid down by the Granard competitions; it is in the second half that the major innovation of the Belfast meeting is stated; a serious attempt is to be made to transcribe the airs, or at least 'the most beautiful and interesting' of them. The ordering of the sentence appears to give the words precedence over the music, an apparent reversal of the order of importance, unless its social significance is appreciated. The 'person well versed in the language' would almost certainly be a gentleman, the 'skilful musician' equally certainly would not (see above, Chapter 3, Notes 23 and 24). The final paragraph articulates and joins together in a potent alliance two of the themes of early romanticism in many parts of Europe, an antiquarian interest in 'national' music and a dawning perception of a possible link between such music and emergent nationalism. The handbill uses it to enlarge and broaden its primary purpose, which is to attract financial contribution. Of those outside Belfast, one of those whom it succeeded in attracting was John O'Neill of Shane's Castle, described by Sir Jonah Barrington as 'one of the most perfect models of an aristocratic patriot',[6] who was prepared to send his organist to help transcribe the music.

A few months later, on Monday 23 April 1792, a meeting of 'several subscribers' took place in the Donegall Arms. A note of the meeting is held in the Linen Hall Library, written on the back of a copy of the handbill of December 1791.[7] There would be an organising committee of five subscribers: they were Henry Joy, Robert Bradshaw, Robert Simms, Dr James McDonnell and John Scott; Robert Bradshaw would be treasurer and secretary.[8] A committee of judges was appointed, and the commencing date of the meeting declared as Tuesday 10 July. The judges included Henry Joy, Robert Bradshaw and Dr McDonnell from the organising committee, together with Rev Mr Meade, Rev Mr Vance, Rainey Maxwell and Thomas Morris Jones, and six women – the Honourable Mrs Meade, the Honourable Miss De Courcy, Mrs McKenzie, Miss Catherine Clarke, Miss Grant and Mrs John Clarke.[9]

Five 'premiums' were decided upon, the sums left blank in the handwritten note but announced in the *Northern Star* (14–18 July 1792) to be 'from ten to two guineas each, according to their different degrees of merit'.[10] Stringent instructions were issued to the judges. 'In order to revive obsolete Airs', the airs were to be confined 'to the native music of the Country, the Music of Ireland', and the judges

> were not to be solely governed in their decisions by the degree of execution or taste of the several performers, but, independently of these

> circumstances, to consider the person entitled to additional claim who shall produce airs not to be found in any public collection, and at the same time deserving of preference by their intrinsic excellence.

Any harper 'in possession of such scarce compositions' was advised to have them 'reduced to notes'. The Reverend Andrew Bryson of Dundalk would be asked to assist, as a person 'versed in the language and antiquities of the Nation'.[11] Mr William Weare [*sic*], Mr Edward Bunting and Mr John Sharpe would be requested to attend as 'practical musicians'. Notification of the date of the meeting and an invitation to harpers to attend would be placed in the Belfast newspapers, the National (Dublin) Journal, and in the newspapers of Cork, Limerick, Waterford, Kilkenny, Galway, Sligo and Derry.

The success of the event, and its blanket coverage in the newspapers, justified the enterprise of the organisers. Despite the widespread advertising, the same small numbers as at Granard competed and the same harpers won the prizes. The decision to have the airs taken down for preservation had been vindicated; to rescue the national music in any substantial way more was needed than competitions. However, in committing themselves not only to transcribing the ancient harp music but to 'arranging' it, the organisers were in effect acknowledging the difficulty of giving it the widest dissemination – if the instrument of transmission was to be the Irish harp. Even if a vogue for that instrument could be created in the population at large, there were constraints upon its development and expansion. The few surviving professional harpers could only spread their talents thinly as performers, and even if they had taken pupils systematically they could not have provided an adequate teaching service. The amateur music-lover had much greater difficulty in acquiring a performing knowledge of the Irish harp than of such popular instruments as flute, violin and piano. This was compounded by the relative scarcity of the instrument itself. There was no substantial market structure for turning out an adequate supply of new instruments: they could not be produced on anything like the scale of the popular instruments. If the Irish harp, then, could not be made in quantity, and few harpers survived to teach it, the music must be preserved in a form accessible to its new guardians, that is to say, in arrangement for other instruments. The few previous collectors of the national music had arranged it for the flute or the violin. That it should be arranged for the instruments familiar to educated society was self-evident; it was also a logical enough conclusion for a society which perceived the traditional music not as a separate music but as part of the European mainstream.[12]

It seems that the Reverend Bryson, Ware and Sharp did not attend, since none of them is mentioned anywhere in the press coverage. The inclusion of John Sharp is interesting as showing the continuing interest of John O'Neill, by now a viscount, in Belfast musical life. As O'Neill's organist at Randalstown and tutor of O'Neill's private band, Sharp was probably a busy enough man already. Also, he had only been resident at Shane's Castle for less than four years,[13] and must have been aware how little contact he had had with traditional Irish music. William Ware, knowing himself to be indifferently qualified for so specialised a role, and able with his customary astuteness to see what a consumer of time and energy it might be, and possibly also what a political dimension it might acquire, left the task to his assistant. Edward Bunting had no choice. Now a young man of nineteen, he was in no position to decline the invitation if he wanted to pursue an adult career in music with the good report of the Belfast townspeople.

Either of the two senior musicians would no doubt have made a professional transcription, selection and arrangement of the music played, to the satisfaction of the organisers.[14] What such a selection might have contained will never be known. Edward Bunting was no stranger to traditional music;[15] yet the music of the harpers was a revelation to him, and the manner in which he was ultimately to deal with it far transcended what could have been in the minds of most if not all of the organisers. He took to his recording task with a will. He was much impressed with the music itself and with its manner of execution; Dennis Hempson, the oldest of the harpers, who played with long crooked nails (see page 44) impressed him most as being the least affected by fashion in music:

> He was the only one who played the very old – the aboriginal – music of the country; and this he did in a style of such finished excellence as persuaded the Editor that the praises of the old Irish harp in Cambrensis – and others – were in reality no more than a just

Denis Hempson, harper,

from BUNTING 1809

tribute to that admirable instrument and its then professors.[16]

Realising that many of the tunes played were already known, and sensing that the harpers, if important, were by no means the only source of the ancient music, Bunting travelled into the countryside to hear the airs if possible where they were still performed, spending long periods first in counties Derry and Tyrone and later in Connacht.[17] Thereafter, by no means the first nor the last scholar to have his joy in research blunted by the subsequent demands of collation, revision and preparation for publication, he was fortunate in having enthusiastic and knowledgeable supporters constantly at his back. The Belfast Society for Promoting Knowledge (now the Linen Hall Library) at its meeting of 7 March 1793 records:

> It having been reported to the committee that a collection of old Irish Musick superior to any hitherto published, was made at the late meeting of the Harpers at Belfast, resolved that it be recommended to the society, to take said work under its patronage, to publish it in London under the name of the Society with a prefatory discourse allowing the profits derived therefrom to the person who took down the notes.[18]

With due acknowledgment of the part played by his supporters, for Edward Bunting to have got his first collection into print in four years, devising his methodology as he went along, was a remarkable achievement.

Subsequent criticism of Bunting has left him to some extent in the position of exasperated veneration accorded by classical archaeologists to Schliemann's excavations at Troy.[19] Yet, although he had no quarrel with the principle of 'arrangement', there was no conscious ignoring on Bunting's part of the special character of the music, rather the contrary. He was cautioned by the organisers against adding a single note to the old melodies,[20] and nearly half a century later was declaring his chief aim to have been 'to guard the primitive air with a religious veneration'.[21] However, if the music which was the subject of his researches would be found by later collectors to have an integrity of its own, alongside but not within the musical systems of the European mainstream in which Bunting had been taught and made his living, he did not see it so. His own choice of the piano derived in part from a conviction that the ancient music was not a separate music. It was a conviction to which he would adhere all the way through his three collections. In his first collection he found that

> the beauty and regularity with which the tunes are constructed

> appear surprising. This circumstance seemed the more extraordinary, when it was discovered that the most ancient tunes were in this respect the most perfect, admitting of the addition of a bass with more facility than such as were less ancient. Hence we may conclude that their authors must have been excellent performers, versed in the scientific part of their profession, and that they had originally a view to the addition of harmony in the composition of their pieces.[22]

In his second collection he drew on a comparison with Wales derived from Gerald of Wales and others:

> If, then, Wales in the tenth and eleventh centuries was in possession of counterpoint and musical notation, it is not to be questioned that the Irish, whose superior knowledge they admitted, by submitting to be taught by them, and to have a body of musical institutes prepared by their direction, could not have been ignorant of either … It has been said that the oldest Irish tunes are the most perfect, and history accords with this opinion … Fuller, in his account of the [first] crusade conducted by Godfrey of Boulogne, says, 'Yes, we might well think that all the concert of Christendom in this war would have made no music if the Irish Harp had been wanting'…[23]

In his final collection he was still adamant:

> the air called 'Ballinderry' … bears unequivocal marks of a very high antiquity, and at the same time possesses the extraordinary peculiarity of a very nearly regular bass called the *Cronan*, running concurrent with the melody through the entire composition. The Editor therefore conceives himself well justified in drawing the conclusion, that those expressions of Cambrensis and others intimate, as plainly as words can, that the Irish of their time had a knowledge of counterpoint, or music in consonance … a fact honourable to Irish music, and the establishment of which gives the Editor a satisfaction that antiquaries might envy.[24]

Bunting's labours on his first volume must have left him little enough time for his work as assistant organist in St Anne's. If Ware had perceived the need for an apprentice to help him in the early 1780s, the need for assistance was at least as great in the expanding town of the 1790s. Ware himself, with the re-establishment of the boarding school under his second wife, the move out of town to Sea View and the increasing, if welcome, demands of the piano boom, had his hands full. Both Ware and Bunting were also encountering the stresses of living in a town, and in an Ireland, which was sliding towards open rebellion. Belfast had been known for most of the century for its radicalism, and attracted a proportionate share of governmental suspicion and attention, overt and covert. What the vicar of St Anne's, who was sovereign of Belfast for seven of the ten years of the decade, thought of the attention to their duties of his organist and assistant organist is not recorded but can hardly have been complimentary. What can be said is that, St Anne's and the ancient music apart, the prime position which Ware enjoyed in Belfast musical life at large had passed to Edward Bunting well before the end of the decade.

NOTES

1 *BN-L*, 16 February 1738.
2 BUNTING 1840, pp. 67-82.
3 *BN-L*, 19 November 1762.
4 It is worth noting in the interest of historical accuracy that what has become generally known as a festival was described in the handbill, in the note of the subsequent meeting of the subscribers, in the contemporary newspaper reports, and in the minutes of the Belfast Society for Promoting Knowledge, as a 'meeting'. For that matter, each Granard competition had been described as a 'ball', and the Three Choirs annual meetings in England were not described as festivals until the nineteenth century. Bunting still calls the 1792 festival a 'meeting' in his 1840 volume, and it is not called a festival in Petrie, *Bunting*, of 1847.
5 A handbill dated Belfast December 1791, of which a copy survives in the Beath MSS, held in the Linen Hall Library. It is quoted in full in Fox, *Annals*, pp. 97–8, in BUNTING 1840, pp. 62–3, and, of more recent commentators, in JOHN KILLEN, *A History of the Linen Hall Library 1788–1988* (Belfast, Linen Hall Library, 1990), p. 173.
6 Quoted in the article on John O'Neill in *Dictionary of National Biography*, (London, Smith, Elder, 1885–1900) vol. xiv, pp. 1092–3.
7 Beath MSS, held in the Linen Hall Library. I am indebted to John Killen for showing me this primary source, part of which he has later reproduced as an illustration in his history of the Library.
8 Fox (*Annals*, pp. 98–99) apparently following *BN-L*, omits the name of John Scott, without substitution, and the appointment of Robert Bradshaw as treasurer and secretary.
9 Fox (*Annals*, p. 99) adds the names of Miss Bristow and Mrs Kennedy.
10 Bunting's recollection, however, is that Charles Fanning was awarded 10 guineas, Arthur O'Neill 8 and 6 to each of the others: BUNTING 1840, p. 64.
11 Fox (*Annals*, p. 99n.) says that he was minister at the presbyterian church of Fourtowns, between Dundalk and Newry (*recte* between Banbridge and Newry) and that 'the presbyterian community being sparse in this district', he had 'leisure for study and literary work'.
12 The conviction was not confined to Ireland. In Scotland, at the time when the Belfast festival was being announced, George Thomson was about to embark on his ambitious plan for Scottish folk melodies. He had developed a taste for Scottish folksongs in mainstream arrangements by hearing foreign singers perform them at the Edinburgh Musical Society concerts (notably the castrato Tenducci, who was well known also in Ireland). Folksongs in their native state, such as he must have heard in his childhood, did not appeal to him. He decided to publish a collection of Scottish folksongs arranged by the greatest living European composers. Pursuing his aim with energy over several decades, he was to persuade many composers, among them Beethoven, who wrote him

126 arrangements, and Haydn, 187. They are still occasionally to be heard, as recital curiosities.

13 He announced his arrival in *BN-L*, 9–12 September 1788.

14 It was considerable in volume. BUNTING 1840, preface, pp. 63–4, lists under the name of each harper the tunes he or she played, and then gives a further list, unattributed to individual players, of other tunes played, 'forming a portion of those airs held in the greatest esteem by the harpers', a grand total of fifty-three.

15 One of the melodies in his 1840 volume, 'O white Maive', is described by him as 'very ancient, author and date unknown, procured from Kitty Doo at Armagh 1780', that is, when he was three years of age: BUNTING 1840, Index to the Airs, p. ix.

16 BUNTING 1840, preface, p. 3.

17 BUNTING 1840, preface, p. 4.

18 The minutes of the Society, held in the Linen Hall Library, record the painstaking and ultimately successful negotiations with Bunting and the publisher in London to get the collection into print. For the efforts of Dr McDonnell in particular see JOHN MAGEE, *The heritage of the harp: the Linen Hall Library and the preservation of Irish music* (Belfast, Linen Hall Library, 1992), *passim*. That the interest continued long after publication of the first volume, see MAGEE and also JOHN KILLEN, 'John Templeton, the Linen Hall Library and the Preservation of Irish Music' in JOHN GRAY and WESLEY McCANN (eds), *An uncommon bookman: essays in memory of J.R.R. Adams* (Belfast, Linen Hall Library, 1996), pp. 199–212.

19 See GEORGE PETRIE, *The Petrie collection of the ancient music of Ireland* (Dublin, Dublin University Press, 1855), pp. xiv–xv, and for modern statements of the defects in his method, GRAINNE YEATS, *The harp of Ireland* (Belfast, Belfast Harpers' Bicentenary, 1992), pp. 26–31 and BREANDÁN BREATHNACH, *Folk music and dances of Ireland* (Cork, Mercier Press, 1971, revised edition 1977), pp. 106–7.

20 BUNTING 1796, preface, unpaginated.

21 BUNTING 1840, preface, p. 6.

22 BUNTING 1796, preface.

23 BUNTING 1809, pp. 7–8.

24 BUNTING 1840, preface, p. 8.

5
CONCERTS IN THE 1790s

'We eat, drink, chat sometimes a little warmly, just as during the American war – but not so as to either interrupt good neighbourhood or our whist.'

(Mrs McTier to William Drennan, 27 February 1793: JEAN AGNEW (ed.), *The Drennan-McTier letters* (3 volumes, Dublin, The Women's History Project in association with Irish Manuscripts Commission, 1998–99), no. 410, vol. 1, p. 496)

IN THE TEMPER OF THE TIMES, concert life was at a standstill. Ware had burnt his fingers in concert promotion and was not inclined to try again. If while he was living at Sea View he was leaving the field to his assistant, the assistant was frequently absent himself on his forays in quest of the ancient music. Significantly, however, the continuing interest created by the harpers' festival made Bunting's researches the stuff of music conversation where his concert prowess, like Ware's, was little mentioned. Public performances of music were few and far between, and the custom of attending them had lapsed. For public amusement there was now only the theatre, hazardous enough on occasion, and the processions and rallies of the garrison and militia. Refuge was taken in private assemblies and coteries. What few public performances there were needed no locally-based organiser.

During the harpers' festival, three experienced professionals, en route from the Rotunda concerts in Dublin to Edinburgh, gave concerts in the Exchange Rooms on two of the evenings after the harpers had stopped for the day. The *Belfast News-Letter*, reporting in enthusiastic detail the first day of the festival, added a final brief paragraph, to the effect that the evening 'produced an exhibition in a very different style, and perhaps less directed to the heart', in a concert given by three artists.[1] They were Joseph Reinagle, a cellist; John Mahon, playing an instrument of his own invention, the *voce clara*, probably of the clarinet family; and Louise Gautherot, doubly notable as a French émigrée and a female virtuoso violinist.[2] The tickets were to be had only at the lodgings of the three soloists; they gave their concerts on their own initiative.

To his credit, Michael Atkins kept his theatre going for quite long periods, despite the fact that the social division of the house into pit, boxes and gallery led all too frequently to the expression of political antagonisms. The only concert advertised in 1793 was the benefit of a singing actress in the theatre company, Mrs Stewart. It took place in the Exchange Rooms, 'instrumental parts by amateurs of the town and the military band', after the premature end of the theatre season;[3] her benefit proper in the new, beleaguered theatre a few weeks earlier[4] had presumably suffered from failing houses in the general atmosphere of disturbance. A total absence of concerts in 1794 was followed by no less than four in 1795. One was given in the theatre, off-season, to show off another singing actress, Miss Bowles 'from the Theatres Royal of Bath and Edinburgh'.[5] A few months later, performances with a musical content were given by two widely travelled showmen. One was John Cartwright, who played the musical glasses,[6] and had added his 'Philosophical Fireworks' to the exhibitions he gave three times a week during the month of October in the George Inn in North Street.[7] The other was the flamboyant dwarf who styled himself 'Count' Boruslavski (the name is variously spelt) and played the guitar.[8] In London in 1783 he had appeared in Polish dress and changed during the interval into the garb of an English gentleman;[9] an impolitic action if he repeated it in the Belfast of 1795.

In the week before Christmas came a flicker of the former concert life. In a concert in the Exchange Rooms Mrs Mahon sang, John Mahon played first violin and also performed on the clarinet and *voce clara*, and Bunting played the piano; the Mahons were on their way between Edinburgh and Dublin.[10] In May 1796 'Mr Shannon from

EXCHANGE-ROOMS, BELFAST.

BY PERMISSION OF GEN. DRUMMOND

MESSRS. BIANCHI and HAIGH, reſpectfully inform the Ladies and Gentlemen of Belfaſt and its Vicinity, they are arrived from Dublin, and intend having a Grand Concert of VOCAL and INSTRUMENTAL MUSIC: On FRIDAY next at the above Rooms.

The have engaged the Muſical Phœnomenon, Maſter MORAN, (a Child only nine years of age), whoſe performance has been the admiration of all the Muſical World.

ACT I.—The celebrated overture to Lodoiſka.—Glee—" How merrily we live that Soldiers be, Mr. ESTE.

Concerto Piano Forte, Maſter Moran, KRUMPHOLTZ.

Song—" Within a Mile of Edinburgh," Mr. Webbe, from the Concerts, Dublin.—Solo Violoncello, Mr. Haigh, in which will be introduced a popular Air, HAIGH.

ACT II.—Glee—" Adieu to the Village Delights."—Duett Violin and Violoncello, Meſſrs. Bianchi and Haigh, GIONOVICHI.—Cramer's celebrated Sonata, Piano Forte, Maſter Moran, in which is introduced the " River Dee," and " Viva tutti."—Hunting Song, Mr. Webbe, " Diana and Hebe."—Concerto Violin, Mr. Bianchi, in which he will introduce " Katty Flannagan," and " Lullaby," BIANCHI—Finale—God ſave the King.

AFTER THE CONCERT A BALL.

The Concert to begin at Eight o'Clock.—Tickets 3s. 9½d. each, to be had of Meſſrs. Bianchi and Haigh, at Mr. Bellew's, High-ſtreet, Mrs. Smyth, Coffee-Houſe, and at the News-Letter Office.

Advertisement of the first concert in the Bianchi-Haigh series: *Belfast News-Letter*, 16 July 1799

Covent Garden', engaged at the theatre to play the Irish pipes, advertised a benefit concert and ball in the Exchange Rooms; no other musicians were mentioned.[11] The only concert advertised in 1797 was to take place in the theatre on 3 July, 'principal vocal part, Mr Harris'; no other musicians were mentioned, and the concert was 'by desire of General Lake',[12] commander of the army in Ireland, who in May 1798 put the country under martial law, the edict accompanied by advice specific to Belfast from his northern commander, General Nugent.[13] Curfew between nine in the evening and five in the morning continued during that summer. Michael Atkins could not put on a season of plays, but in the early days of November, giving good notice, he advertised a concert, to be given in the theatre on Saturday 1 December, beginning at six and finishing before curfew at nine.[14] By early spring of 1799, when things had eased, two guitar recitals were advertised in April for the Exchange Rooms by Count Boruslavski.[15]

At last, in July 1799, there came the first advertisement of a series of concerts which was to run until the end of September. Two Dublin-based musicians, J.M.C. Bianchi, leader of the band at the Crow Street theatre, and Robert Haigh, a cellist, were the promoters and they had with them a pianist, Master Moran, aged nine, and a singer, Mr Webbe, described as from the concerts in Dublin.[16] The season consisted of five concerts in the Exchange Rooms and one in the theatre. They were remarkable not only for the standard and consistency of programme and for their comprehensive advertisements, but also for the manner in which the visitors accepted help from, and identified with, the local musicians. The concert on Friday 16 August[17] began with an overture followed by a glee. In the piano concerto to be played by Master Moran the composer's name (Krumpholtz) was given. Bianchi was named as the composer of his violin concerto, which in the fashion of the time introduced named airs, as did Master Moran's solo by Cramer. The second concert included Haydn's 'celebrated Surprise', a sonata by Corelli and a Clementi 'lesson for the piano forte'.[18] In the third concert there was a piano concerto played by Bunting (no composer named) and Master Moran played Pleyel's 'German Hymn' (a popular arrangement of a movement from a Pleyel string quartet). Webbe sang a duet with 'an amateur'.[19] It was probably the degree of local assistance available, vocal as well as instrumental, that encouraged Bianchi and Haigh to advertise as the final item 'Handel's Grand Chorus of the Coronation Anthem'. The concert on Tuesday 27 August was for the benefit of the Poor House and Infirmary[20] and included a Pleyel quartet, in which Bianchi and Haigh were to be joined by Coleman and Bunting, presumably as second violin and viola. J.H. Coleman's plaintive advertisement had appeared in the previous year:

> Music master, lately from London, where he performed on the piano forte and violin … offers himself as a teacher of those instruments … tunes harpsichords and piano fortes … during a residence of nine

> years at Gibraltar, studied under the famous Jardine [Giardini?] and others. The circumstance of his father dying in the army while in the West Indies, where he lost all his property, and having him (now only seventeen years of age) the sole support of a mother and five children, will, he hopes, be an additional recommendation to the ladies and gentlemen of Belfast and its neighbourhood.[21]

Bunting's piano sonata, obviously of his own composition, would introduce an (unnamed) 'ancient Irish air'.

The *Belfast News-Letter* of 27 August had three musical events advertised in two adjoining columns. One was for the Poor House concert. Another was for Master Moran's benefit concert to be held a week later. The third was for an event of some note in St Anne's, which was occasioned by the presence of the visiting musicians and which drew together several important strands in the life of Belfast at that time.

An important extension of the work of the Charitable Society was the medical dispensary which Dr James McDonnell had helped to found in 1792. Attended by no great initial success, it had been reorganised in 1797 as a house with six beds in Factory Row with a nurse, a resident apothecary, and Dr McDonnell as one of the two attending physicians, under the name of 'The Belfast Dispensary and Fever Hospital'.[22] The charity sermon in 1799 was in aid of the fund set up to establish it: 'it is hoped no person will attend who does not mean in some degree to contribute'.[23] Persuaded no doubt by his organist and assistant organist, Rev William Bristow took the opportunity to give his parishioners a cathedral service, to be performed 'by several musical gentlemen, who have kindly offered their assistance on this occasion'. After sermon and service, there would be 'a Grand Selection[24] of Sacred Music, from the *Messiah* and other Oratorios by Handel'. There were listed 'Comfort ye' and 'Every valley', 'And the glory', 'For unto us', 'I know that my Redeemer liveth' and 'Hallelujah'; so was 'Angels ever bright and fair' from *Theodora*. The vocal parts would be taken by 'Messrs Webb, Bianchi, Haigh, Ware, Barr,[25] etc etc' and the organ played, 'with a Voluntary', by Bunting. The concert in the theatre was Master Moran's benefit on Tuesday 3 September,[26] with the 'German Hymn' again and 'The Battle of Prague' as well as Lord Mornington's popular glee, 'Here in cool grot'.

Master Moran's name does not occur in the advertised programme of the final concert, to be held in the Exchange Rooms on Wednesday 18 September, postponed for some reason until Monday 23.[27] It was the benefit concert for Bianchi, Haigh and Webbe. Bunting performed a piano concerto with an ancient Irish air. The evening began with a Haydn symphony and ended with the Hallelujah Chorus. Haigh contributed a new cello concerto; he and Bianchi played a duet and Bianchi a violin concerto.[28] There was a new glee, 'The Red Cross knight' by Callcott. Also in the first half were the first and second parts of 'the original recitatives, songs and choruses in *Macbeth*, composed by M. Locke'; placed between Bunting's and Bianchi's concertos in the second half was the final part. It was familiar music – the tragedy was rarely performed without it – but its inclusion, separated into parts, was an interesting exercise in programme planning.[29] With a ball afterwards the series ended.

Before they left Belfast the visitors put two separate notices in the same edition of a newspaper. The first read:

> Messrs Bianchi, Haigh and Webb return thanks for support of their concerts. They cannot pass over the assistance they have received from their brother performers in this town.

The second had reverberations all the way back to the concert visitors of half a century before, even to the use of the verb 'encourage':

> Mr Webb having been encouraged to remain in this part of the country for some time to give instructions in singing assures the public of their satisfaction…[30]

and instead of quoting eminent teachers and triumphs in other places, he simply said 'for his abilities refer to Messrs Ware and Bunting'.

What induced Bianchi and Haigh, not household names like Ashe and Mahon, to come to Belfast in the summer of 1799 is not known, but the imminence of the passing the Act of Union, under which Ireland was to be governed directly from London, may have caused some Dublin-based musicians to survey other fields. It was to be expected that the dissolution of the Irish parliament would be followed by the departure of many of the nobility and gentry, with their personal entourages and supporting bureaucracy, and that with the reduction of patronage opportunities for musicians would be reduced. In practice the abruptness of the change was mitigated by the facts that the middle classes had begun to form a significant element of the Dublin concert public before the Act of Union, and that substantial powers remained vested in Dublin Castle after it.[31] Bianchi died in Paris three years later, still in his middle twenties.[32] As has been seen, Webbe announced an intention to stay in Belfast and teach singing. In 1800 Michael Atkins engaged Haigh to conduct the orchestra in the theatre.[33] In 1801 he was at work in the theatre and making concert appearances as a cellist. In September 1801 he announced that he had decided to live in Belfast and teach.[34] Thereafter, up to and including 1811, with few gaps, Haigh appears in newspaper advertisements as having at least one benefit per season, the normal reward for a season's work. Only the young Patrick Moran can be traced as having returned to Dublin; he made a career there as pianist and composer.[35]

If, as the century came to a close, the political climate at home and abroad were to allow subscription concerts to resume, they could do so on a new basis of mutual respect between local and visiting professionals, with an audience increasing as the town grew in size and the commercialisation of leisure gained in pace. Better land and sea communications were making Belfast easier of access, and its placing on the travel route between Dublin and Scotland was gaining in use and importance. Edward Bunting, now an established professional musician, was engaged on the research for his second volume of the ancient music. He was also ready to take up a career as a mainstream musician based on the post of church organist he had been trained for. The militancy of radical politics did not cease in Ireland with the suppression of the 1798 rebellion, but the abortive revolt a few years later associated with the name of Robert Emmet had nothing like the public support in the north of Ireland enjoyed by the United Irishmen in their early years. Belfast remained, however, a town under official suspicion. Bunting had to watch his step: his friendship with Thomas Russell, who was to be hanged as a rebel, was no secret. His colleague Patrick Lynch working in Connacht found himself suspected as one on some secret mission from Belfast. I could not get many songs in Westport on account of this report; for the persons from whom I expected them were afraid to be seen in my company.[36]

NOTES

1 *BN-L*, 10–13 July 1792.
2 A London professional, voicing the prejudice against the unseemliness of a lady playing the violin, said 'Madam Gautherot, from Paris, performed ... a concerto on the violin with great ability. The ear, however, was more gratified than the eye by this lady's masculine effort': W.T. PARKE, *Musical memoirs* (2 volumes, London, Colburn and Bentley, 1830), vol. 1, p. 129.
3 *NS*, 5–8 June 1793. Atkins opened his new theatre in Arthur Street in February and had to close it at the end of May because of persistent disturbances; he deemed it imprudent to reopen until September 1794.
4 *BN-L*, 7–10 May 1793.
5 *BN-L*, 29 June–3 July 1795.
6 The musical glasses, after Benjamin Franklin's radical improvements, became a sophisicated instrument known as the 'armonica' for which Mozart wrote a quintet, K. 617. Cartwright's earlier visit to Belfast in 1770 had occurred in the middle of the instrument's vogue.
7 *BN-L/NS*, October 1795, *passim*.
8 *NS*, 22–26 October 1795.
9 SIMON MCVEIGH, *Concert life in London from Mozart to Haydn* (Cambridge, Cambridge University Press, 1993), p. 85.
10 *NS*, 10–14 December 1795.
11 *NS*, 9–13 May 1796.
12 *BN-L*, 30 June 1797.
13 *BN-L*, 29 June–3 July 1795.
14 *BN-L*, 7 November 1798.
15 *BN-L*, 2, 9 April 1799.
16 *BN-L*, 16 July 1799. For a discussion of the identities of Bianchi and Haigh see T.J. WALSH, *Opera in Dublin 1798–1820* (Oxford, Oxford University Press, 1993), p. 16; ROY JOHNSTON, *Concerts in the musical life of Belfast to 1874* (unpublished PhD thesis, Queen's University Belfast, 1996), pp. 234–235; DEREK COLLINS, *Concert life in Dublin in the Age of Revolution*, (unpublished PhD thesis, Queen's University Belfast, 2001), pp. 143–144.
17 *BN-L*, 16 July 1799.
18 *BN-L*, 2, 6 August 1799.
19 *BN-L*, 16 August 1799.
20 *BN-L*, 27 August 1799.
21 *BN-L*, 5 October 1798.
22 PETER FROGGATT, 'Dr James McDonnell, M.D., 1763–1845', *The Glynns: Journal of the Glens of Antrim Historical Society*, 9, 1981, p. 23.
23 *BN-L*, 27 August 1799.
24 In a church the term 'concert' was avoided.
25 Henry Barr was another Armagh-trained musician working in Belfast.
26 *BN-L*, 30 August 1799.

27 *BN-L*, 13, 17 September 1799.

28 The absence of composers' names of concertos probably indicates that, as was still common at the time, they were composed by the solo performer. Master Moran's concertos are by named composers, either because the custom was passing or because he was not deemed capable at his tender age of composing his own. It was the custom also for most composers, whether in concertos or other worked-out compositions, to use folk melodies as thematic material. It would be interesting to know if Bunting's 'ancient Irish airs' were from his own collection; the fact that no such reference is made may be an indication that the airs of his first collection, however locally esteemed, had not made their way into concert repertoire; the ancient music of Ireland was not a central feature of the emerging concert life of Belfast.

29 The music is now known to be by Richard Leveridge.

30 *BN-L*, 1 October 1799.

31 COLLINS, *Thesis*, pp. 24–6.

32 WALSH, *Opera in Dublin 1798–1820*, p. 16.

33 *BN-L*, 5 December 1800.

34 *BN-L*, 1 September 1801.

35 ITA HOGAN, *Anglo-Irish music 1780–1830* (Cork, Cork University Press, 1966), p. 204.

36 Patrick Lynch in Westport to John McCracken in Belfast, 21 June 1802: *BUNTING MSS* 4/35/33.

6
THE NEW CENTURY

'We cannot overlook the advanced state of Music within the last 15 or 20 years. Instead of the number of instruments being limited to a very few, there are now few genteel families in which that delightful art has not been introduced as a necessary female accomplishment. Under the directing taste of one of the best performers in this kingdom on the Organ and Piano Forte, *Subscription Concerts* have been instituted by a few gentlemen, on a plan as extensive and liberal as is compatible with a select and genteel auditory ... The musical world has been already indebted to the professional gentleman alluded to, for the first part of a collection of the most ancient airs of a nation famed through Europe from the earliest ages for the melody of the Harp.'

Belfast News-Letter, 21 May 1805

THE EFFECT ON BELFAST'S MUSICAL LIFE of these years of conflict and change at home and abroad was not entirely deleterious: an enhanced sensitivity to music in time of national distress is a well-attested commonplace, and within Belfast itself two musical initiatives of importance were to take place before the fall of Napoleon.

Much of Edward Bunting's energy in the mid-1790s had been directed to the production of his first collection. In the new century William Ware took a back seat. For most of the first two decades of the nineteenth century the musical life of Belfast was dominated by Edward Bunting, his activity as performer and concert promoter backed by the prestige he had gained from his published work on the ancient music. In the first decade, the preparation of his second collection took up an increasing amount of his time.

In the immediate aftermath of the Bianchi/Haigh concerts the promise of enhanced concert activity seems not to have been realised. The theatre in April 1800 had a topical afterpiece called *A Ramble through Belfast.*[1] The eight scenes included 'Rooms on a Coterie Night, Music, Taste etc' and 'A Peep into the Playhouse, Actors, Critics etc', but no mention of concerts. Bunting's name as concert promoter does not appear until March 1801 when he and Haigh put on a concert for the hospital.[2] Master Owens, lately arrived in town with his father,[3] played a violin concerto by Giornovichi. He was in the company of Bunting himself playing a piano concerto, of a bandmaster playing a clarinet concerto, of Haigh with a cello solo, and of Michael Atkins' daughter Mrs Boucheron singing a song by Haigh. The accounts of the beneficiaries, published later in the year, included the considerable sum of £50 3s 1d.[4]

Shortly after the end of the 1800-01 season Bunting announced a series of eight pre-season subscription concerts conducted by himself in the Donegall Arms, to commence on 25 July.[5] The principal performers named were Haigh, Owens and the Dublin-based harpist Seybold. Taking a leaf out of Ware's book, he also persuaded a famous visitor, the English tenor Charles Incledon, engaged at the theatre, to sing in St Anne's on Sunday 2 August on the occasion of a charity sermon for the Poor House and Infirmary.[6] The church service was followed by music from the oratorios of Handel; Incledon and the soprano Mrs Addison were the soloists. Since Haigh is described as principal cello, Bunting at the organ may have had the assistance of a band or instrumental group in the solos, choruses and anthems and in the overture to *Messiah*. It was perhaps Bunting who promoted Mrs Addison's concert and ball on 15 August, since it was the date of one of his subscription concerts.[7] Only Mrs Addison and Seybold were named, but it seems reasonable to suppose that the piano concerto was played by Bunting and that Haigh played with Master Owens in the violin-and-cello duet and with Bunting in the piano-and-cello duet.

Towards the end of the series, at the beginning of the season proper, an advertisement appeared which seems to indicate the presence in Belfast of a musical society, independent of Bunting's concerts:

> Private concert. The conductors of the above meeting inform the public that non-subscribers cannot be admitted except by tickets from one of the Gentlemen Performers.[8]

No other mention occurs. A group referred to in much later years comes to mind. In 1839, when Bunting was living in Dublin, the solicitor James Sidebotham gave him active help from London in the publication of his third and final volume. In a letter to Bunting dated 19 July 1839, frequently quoted, enclosing the corrected proofs, he says:

> I am glad that you were able to take a journey to the North. I wish it had been possible for me to have met you there. I don't know anything which would have given me greater pleasure than to visit Belfast, and contemplate those days of old, and our 'merry meetings' at the Commercial Rooms, where with yourself, Moorhead, Bob Haigh, May, Gunning, Soane, Drs Thomson and Magee, we had used to meet every week to *scratch* Haydn and Beethoven.[9]

Sidebotham's memory is at fault: the Commercial Buildings were not opened until 1820, when Bunting had gone to live in Dublin; three of the names are those of successive leaders of the theatre orchestra and it is unlikely that they could have played together. Nevertheless, Sidebotham's recollection, with its imperfections, is vivid enough to indicate the existence of what appears to have been preponderantly, but not exclusively, a professional group; Sloane, Dr Thomson, Dr Magee and the writer were amateurs. The impression given is of a recreational group, a 'private concert' meeting to play music they would be unlikely to meet in their daily activities; but the possibility that they may have also given public concerts by subscription, like the Belfast Musical Society some decades earlier, cannot be ruled out.

In January 1802 there was a brief reference to a series of subscription concerts commencing on Saturday 16th in the Exchange Rooms, subscribers' tickets transferable to ladies only.[10] Nothing appeared in the newspapers as to their progress, but it seems likely that they were Bunting's. Bunting was working on his second collection: there was the publisher to be met and forays made in Ireland to collect airs. He sent Patrick Lynch into Connacht while he went to London himself. He did not do these things, however, until the season in Belfast was coming to an end;[11] he played in Master Owens' benefit concert in the theatre with Haigh, Byrne, Giesler and Coleman on 4 March,[12] and there may have been other concert commitments.

Belfast now had its own nobility around whom to build the social season. From 1802 the marquis and marchioness of Donegall lived in a house on the corner of Donegall Place, and retained it as a town house after moving out in 1807 to Ormeau.[13] There is no evidence of Bunting being brought into the orbit of their favour either as local musician or folksong collector. Anna Walker, wife of the colonel of the West Kent Regiment, kept a diary and recorded her social life in the Belfast of 1802–3. She never refers to having been at a public concert. She was entertained, however, by the marchioness and 'excessively amused by a Miss Draper who played uncommonly well on the harp',[14] and whom she found a few weeks later to be harp tutor to the children of the Londonderry family at Mount Stewart.[15] Unlikely to be an Irish harper (her name is not found in the sources), 'Miss Draper' is more likely to have been the émigrée Mlle Dupré, who had announced her arrival in Belfast, an 'élève of Krumpholtz', to give lessons on the pedal harp and sell Erard's 'celebrated pedal harps'.[16] At her concert in the Exchange Rooms on 12 October, under the patronage of the marchioness of Donegall,[17] she played a concerto, a duet with Bunting and a trio sonata with Master Owens and Haigh; Master Owens also contributed a violin concerto and Bunting a piano concerto.

It is possible that occasionally artists in transit between Dublin and Edinburgh performed in the subscription concerts, their names disseminated in whatever advertising media Bunting may have used instead of the newspapers. When they passed through between seasons, especially when Bunting was not in town, they had to do their own promotion and advertising. The violinist Paul Alday and Peter Urbani, who had sung in Belfast with the Weichsells in 1784, gave a concert in the Exchange Rooms en route to Dublin.[18] 'Madam Dussek' advertised that she would sing and perform on the harp and piano;[19] she was Sophia Corri, the deserted wife of Jan Ladislav Dussek, making a living as a concert artist and en route from Dublin.[20]

Subscription series are not advertised in the season 1802-3 and succeeding seasons, but there is evidence of their existence in at least part of the period in an editorial piece written near the end of the 1804-5 season about general improvements in the quality of life in Belfast, quoted at the head of this chapter. That there were subscription concert series in the early years of this decade, and that they were Bunting's, seems clear from this notice. But evidence is almost totally lacking of their degree of success. It does seem that, unlike Ware, Bunting relied on other means than the public prints to publicise them; even so, on the experience of Ware's and other concerts, one would have expected visiting soloists, who lived by publicity, to have

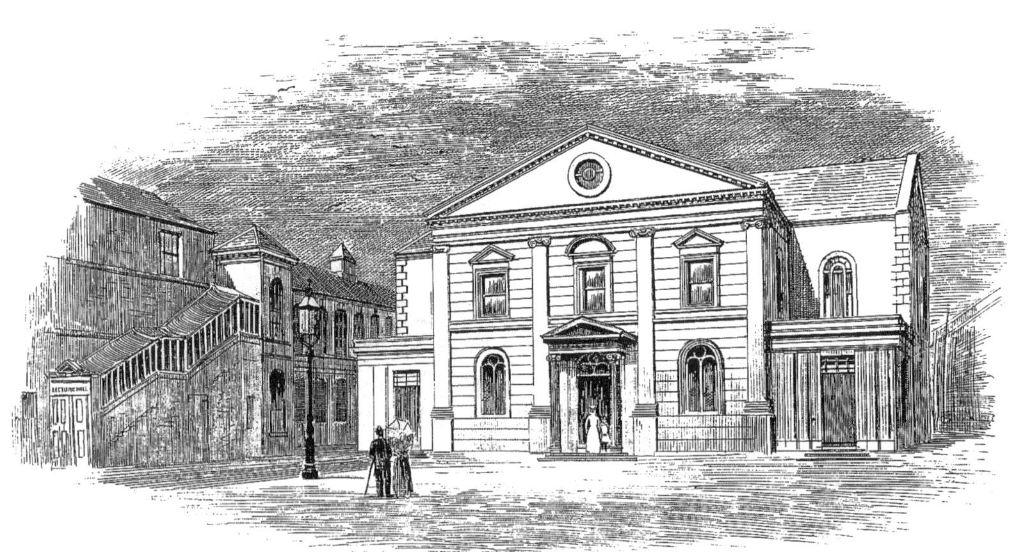

Second Presbyterian Church, 'Dr Drummond's Meeting-House', in Rosemary Street, opened 1790

from Millin's *History of the Second Congregation*

been named. It is possible, at one extreme, that Bunting ran subscription series which were uniformly successful and vindicated his approach to advertisement; at the other, that, as with Ware, some took place and others did not. The notice above seems to favour the former.

It would not be surprising if subscription series ceased after 1805. No-one else seems likely to have promoted them, and Bunting had other pressing matters on his hands. His second collection was a more complicated venture than the first and was to take up more and more of his time over the next four years. Also, having emerged from his apprenticeship with Ware, he had found himself with the choice of staying in a subordinate position in St Anne's – there being no other church in Belfast with an organ – or of becoming an organist in another town. His expertise was eventually to be availed of in Belfast, but outside the anglican tradition. In 1801, he had made a 'very liberal proposal respecting the purchase of an organ' to First Presbyterian church, and had it courteously refused.[21] His initiative was not lost on the new minister of the church next door.[22] The Second Presbyterian congregation of Belfast had replaced their church in 1790 and in 1800 called William Hamilton Drummond to be their minister. Born at Larne in 1778, he was a man of intellectual breadth and energy. He was the youngest member of the Belfast Literary Society on its formation in 1801 and its secretary and president in 1813. Poet and lecturer, he also ran a school for young gentlemen in his house at Mount Collyer. He was twenty-two when he came to Second Presbyterian, and six years later he was within sight of his goal of having an organ. By September 1806 Bunting had a new post:

> Tomorrow, a Charity Sermon will be preached in the Meeting of the Second Congregation of Presbyterians, by the Rev Mr Drummond … This is the first congregation of Protestant Dissenters in the North of Ireland which has introduced an organ into the public worship. It will be played by Mr Edward Bunting … it has been built by Mr White, an ingenious mechanic from London, and is constructed so as to acquire considerable power from the use of pedals.[23]

At a further charity sermon in November,[24] members of the choir of Armagh Cathedral attended (Bunting, like Ware, had maintained an Armagh connection): Kent's anthem 'Hear my prayer' was sung, as well as 'I know that my Redeemer liveth' and the Hallelujah Chorus. The collection was £214 5s 6d, a very high figure.

There was great material benefit to all parties in Second Presbyterian. The congregation had their new organ, and to play it an excellent performer who had also a high reputation as a rescuer of the traditional music. Bunting, in this regard a man of the Belfast of his time, had secured a post in a new enterprise with its way to make, which gave him a degree of independence he would have found it hard to obtain in an anglican church. He was playing on an instrument in the design of which he had no doubt participated. If the music of the presbyterian services was less rich and varied than the anglican, that gave him more time to work on his second volume. Above all, he was sure of the encouragement of his young minister. Bunting's years in Second Presbyterian, and his creative partnership with Dr Drummond, were the high plateau of his professional career. Bunting may have been too busy for subscription concerts in the season, but he brought off a concert coup in September 1807 which transcended anything the concert life of Belfast had yet experienced. It was an opportunist initiative reminiscent of Ware with John Abraham Fisher nearly twenty years earlier:

> MR BUNTING is This Day authorised to inform the Public, from MADAM CATALANI, that in consequence of her arrangements in Dublin permitting her to visit Belfast ONE day sooner than she intended, she will, on THURSDAY the 17th instant, for that NIGHT only, sing in a CONCERT at the Theatre...[25]

The singer of the early nineteenth century who left the most vivid impression upon those who heard her, and who in the early years of her career dominated her period, was the Italian soprano Angelica Catalani. Her voice had volume, strength and astonishing agility. She was also a surpassingly handsome woman. She liked to appear as a queen in the theatre, and as a queen she expected to be treated outside it. Her fees were notoriously monstrous; the blame for this was usually laid to the charge of her husband, Paul Valabrègue, whom she met in Lisbon early in her career when he was a military attaché at the French embassy. On this her first visit to Dublin, Bunting had persuaded her north. She would be assisted by two male singers from London, Rovedino and Morelli. Tom Cooke was coming with them

Angelica Catalani
NATIONAL PORTRAIT GALLERY

from Dublin to lead the band. For such an occasion the house would be lighted with wax and to meet her fees the prices of seats were much higher than usual (boxes half a guinea, pit 8s 9d, gallery 5s 5d). Catalani sang her arias by Portogallo, Mayr and Paisiello. Bunting was

THEATRE, BELFAST.

LAST NIGHT.

MADAME CATALANI,

WILL, on THIS NIGHT, September 19th, 1807, form in a

GRAND CONCERT,

ASSISTED BY

MESSRS. ROVEDINO & MORELLI,

From the Opera-House London.

FIRST ACT,

Symphony..................... *Pleyel.*

Aria, SIGNOR ROVEDINO.......... *Cimarosa.*

Pollacca, MADAME CATALANI......... *Mayer*

Aria, SIGNOR MORELLI...... *Paisiello.*

Duet, SIGNORI ROVEDINO & MORELLI... *Ferrari.*

Grand Aria, Dove il cimento, MADAME CATALANI........... *Cimarosa.*

SECOND ACT.

Aria, SIGNOR ROVEDINO............... *Sacchini.*

Duet (Buffo), from the celebrated Opera of "*IL FANATICO PER LA MUSICA*;"

MADAME CATALANI, & SIGNOR MORELLI.

Concerto Violin, Mr. T. COOKE, in which will be introduced the Air of "*Gramachree Molly*," and (by particular desire) the Polish Rondo.. *Cooke.*

Aria, SIGNOR MORELLI.......... *Mengozi.*

Aria, Nel cor piu nomi Sento,

MADAME CATALANI,

(*With her own Variations.*)

The Band will be led by Mr. T. COOKE, from the Theatre Royal, Dublin.

The Concert, under the direction of Mr. BUNTING, who will preside at the Piano-Forte.

Boxes, Half-a-Guinea—Pit, 8*s*. 9*d*.—and Gallery, 5*s*. 5*d*.—Doors to be opened at Seven o'Clock, the Concert to begin at a Quarter past Eight.

Tickets will be Sold by Messrs. MAGEE, Bridge-street, and ARCHER and HODGSON, High-street, Booksellers; and at the Donegall-Arms.

Mr. WALLACE will, as usual, attend at the Box-Office of the Theatre, from Eleven till Four o'Clock.

It is requested that such Ladies and Gentlemen as have taken Places, will be good enough to send for Tickets in order to prevent confusion at the Doors.

The advertisement of Catalani's second concert in *Belfast Commercial Chronicle* (19 September 1807) praised for the 'judgment and regularity' he displayed in conducting the performance (presumably from the keyboard).[26] Catalani was persuaded to give a second concert two nights later, and this was the occasion of a detailed advertisement.[27] Earlier in the day she had been recognised in the large crowd attending the launch of the 'Eliza', a big new ship for the West Indian trade, at Ritchie's shipyard.[28] The great soprano returned to Ireland the following year, and Bunting succeeded in bringing her to Belfast again, this time to the Exchange Rooms on 24 October 1808. Bunting presided at the piano, Spagnoletti led the band and played a violin concerto, and Guglielmo Catalani, who was Angelica Catalani's brother and a member of the Crow Street theatre band in Dublin, played an oboe solo.[29] But Catalani had overreached herself on this occasion. Her fees had caused Bunting to charge a guinea a seat. There were to have been two concerts, but the uptake of seats justified one only.[30] The single concert attracted a respectable house, for that auditorium, of two hundred. Concert promotion was still a fickle business.

Bunting's first collection of the ancient music had consisted of arranged melodies without words. As work on the second collection of fifty-four airs went on, the Power brothers in Dublin published the first volume of their Irish Melodies. Much of their phenomenal success lay in the original verses of Thomas Moore, and Bunting allowed himself to embark, in emulation, on an ambitious plan of having translations from the Irish made by the most eminent poets of the day. Not having the Irish language himself, his purpose in enlisting the help of Patrick Lynch and despatching him ahead into Connacht was to procure the words in the original, so that they would be available for publication and for translators. It used up a great deal of time and was only partly successful. Twenty airs in the published volume had verses: the Scottish poet Thomas Campbell was to be the big name:

> But, if the well of Campbell's genius ran deep and clear, it was exceedingly difficult to pump anything out of it; and so, after a long delay, and innumerable fruitless applications, Bunting was ultimately obliged to content himself with two indifferent songs, and permission to use two of the poet's ballads, written long previous to the agreement, and which, however excellent they confessedly were, in

> their way, were entirely out of their place in a collection of Irish melodies.[31]

Seven other writers contributed one each, the best known Dr Drennan and Dean Swift; the remaining nine airs had words by Miss Balfour, who ran a school in Belfast in which Bunting taught music. There was no question of matching the popularity of Moore's Melodies, and Bunting had wasted a great deal of time and energy in trying. Expectation was high: in 1807 a 'roundelay' appeared in the press addressed to him; the first of its seven stanzas read:

> Now fair befall thee, Bard!
> Who thus had taste to save
> The simple lays
> Of other days
> From dull oblivion's grave.[32]

The prospectus, issued in the following summer, declared that the collection was now nearly ready for publication 'after a long but necessary delay'.[33] It was not until January 1810 that Bunting received proof copies.[34] A review appeared in London in the March issue of a journal, *Le Beau Monde*; it was reprinted, with Bunting's letter to the editor, in the Belfast press. Stung by the reviewer's assertion that Sir John Stevenson had forestalled him in publishing the 'first general collection of Irish airs', Bunting reminded him of his own 1796 collection and drew a distinction:

> Our respective works move in different spheres, and aim at different objects. One of these consists of tunes generally known in Great Britain and Ireland, forming a *selection* which an able musician could produce in his elbow chair: the other is a *collection*, which embraces similar objects, with the advantage of having every well-authenticated, valuable, and really *ancient* melody that could be restored, by the active exertions of almost my life-time – a Collection, which, at this period, it is out of the power of any other person to make.[35]

Upstaged by Moore and Stevenson abroad, Bunting could take some satisfaction at home in the initial success of the Irish Harp Society. The townspeople who had organised the 1792 festival were gratified with Bunting's work on the music, but the harp and the harper had also to be preserved. In 1808 they established a Harp Society. The contributions of subscribers promised an annual income of £300,[36] on which a scheme was launched under which twelve poor children were to be lodged and fed, and taught the harp by Arthur O'Neill of the 1792 festival. Dr James McDonnell was again a prime mover. Bunting's connection was limited to membership of the committee, but in December 1809 the Society gave a dinner in honour of their 'powerful auxiliary … as a mark of individual respect and public esteem'. After dinner Arthur O'Neill and his pupils, all blind, one a girl, played harp music.[37] Well reported in the press, the Society pressed on with the creation of an administrative structure within which the training of harpers and the study in depth of its music and the Irish language could be pursued.

Although his third collection was not to appear until long after he had left Belfast to live in Dublin, Bunting was far from idle in the years after the publication of his second. He did not resume his subscription concerts, or if he did there is no inkling of them in the newspapers. However, his contribution to the mainstream musical life of Belfast was shortly to reach its zenith. The encomium of 1805 had indicated a significant gap in the musical life of the town.

NOTES

1 *BN-L*, 22 April 1800.
2 *BN-L*, 10 March 1801.
3 *BN-L*, 20 January 1801.
4 *BN-L*, 29 December 1801.
5 *BN-L*, 21 July 1801. His chances of making a profit on concerts in that restricted auditorium must have been small.
6 *BN-L*, 31 July 1801.
7 *BN-L*, 11 August 1801.
8 *BN-L*, 8 September 1801.
9 Reproduced in FOX, *Annals*, pp. 296–7.
10 *BN-L*, 12 January 1802.
11 Lynch, in Drogheda on his way west, wrote on 25 April to Bunting, who was in Belfast preparing to leave for England: FOX, *Annals*, p. 230. His business in England completed, Bunting joined Lynch in Westport on 5 July: FOX, *Annals*, p. 256.
12 *BN-L*, 2 March 1802.
13 W.A. MAGUIRE, 'Lords and landlords – the Donegall family', in BECKETT *et al.*, *Belfast: the making of the city*, pp. 28–29.
14 MRS ANNA WALKER, *Diary 1802–7* (held in the Public Record Office of Northern Ireland), entry of 25 September 1802.
15 WALKER, *Diary*, entry of 26 October 1802.
16 *BN-L*, 2 March 1802.
17 *BN-L*, 1 October 1802.
18 *BN-L*, 3 August 1804.
19 *BN-L*, 16 July 1805.
20 *Faulkner's Dublin Journal*, 8 June 1805.
21 *First Presbyterian Church: congregational minutes 1760* – (held in the church), meeting of 10 May 1801.
22 At this time First, Second and Third Presbyterian churches stood on adjacent sites in Rosemary Street.
23 *Belfast Commercial Chronicle*, 6 September 1806.
24 *BN-L*, 28 November 1806.
25 *BN-L*, 15 September 1807.
26 *BN-L*, 19 September 1807.
27 *BN-L*, 19 September 1807.
28 *BCC*, 21 September 1807.
29 *BCC*, 26 October 1808.
30 *BN-L*, 18 October 1808. Catalani, with her exuberant personality, was always the stuff of anecdote. She prided herself on her grasp of English, and when she met Bunting on her final visit to Ireland, PETRIE (*Bunting*, p. 71) relates the 'curious dialogue which took place between them':

CATALANI. Well, my dear Mr Bunting, how glad I am to see you looking so strong and well.

BUNTING. Ugh, ugh, no, madam. I'm growing fat and lazy like an old dog as I am.

CATALANI. Ah indeed, Mr Bunting, and I too am growing fat and lazy like an old dog as I am – no, that is not the word – like an old bitch, Mr Bunting!

31 PETRIE, *Bunting*, p. 71.

32 *BCC*, 25 February 1807.

33 *BN-L*, 23 August 1808.

34 *BCC*, 20 January 1810. The title page of the published volume gives no date of publication. The plate of Hempson between pp. iii and 1 has the subscript 'London. Published by E Bunting. Novr 1809'.

35 *BCC*, 18 April 1810.

36 *Minutes of the Irish Harp Society* (held in the Linen Hall Library), unpaginated.

37 *BN-L*, 22 December 1809. The many toasts did not include one to Moore or Stevenson – nor to the Dublin Harp Society, inaugurated in July 1809 with Moore and Sir Walter Scott among its subscribers.

7
THE 1813 FESTIVAL

'We will take the liberty to remark, that the introduction of some of Handel's Oratorios would still further improve our musical taste, by leading "the harmony of sweet sounds" to its noblest object and end'.

Belfast News-Letter, 21 May 1805

IN MAY 1813 the Belfast newspapers carried a preliminary anouncement:

MUSICAL FESTIVAL

The improvement of Ulster in the fine arts has for many years been progressive; but it is to be regretted that that province has never had an opportunity of witnessing the power of Music, in the most rational and sublime display of it, *an Oratorio*. This treat is at present in contemplation; being set on foot by an inhabitant of this town, of the highest professional abilities. A *Musical Festival* is in preparation, to be held at Belfast, as the most populous town in the North, upon a similar plan to those which have long attracted public admiration in the principal Cathedrals and chief towns of England. It is to continue a week in the month of *September* next; and the first talents which this kingdom affords are to be collected on the occasion. It is not, however, to be confined to a single oratorio, as that of the *Messiah*, inimitable as it is, but it is also to comprehend selections from Handel's other sacred and his lighter compositions; as also from the

> productions of other masters. By such means, public taste may, in a few days, receive greater improvement in this admirable art than it ever could without them. Pleased with an attempt that promises so much delightful entertainment, this Paper will communicate every information that shall be made to it on the subject. The expence must be great, from the number of eminent performers required; but it gives us pleasure to be informed that the surplus is to be presented to the Managers of the Belfast Poor-House. A greater incentive could not be held out for the exertions of the humane. The encouragement of Noble Families, of Gentlemen and Ladies in distant parts, in *Newry*, *Derry* and *Armagh*, may naturally be expected. In England, where such festivals occur often, they are flocked to from all quarters. Our opportunities are fewer than theirs, but our natural taste for excellence is not, we should hope, less.[1]

Belfast had by this time a population approaching 30,000; dwarfed to insignificance by the 120,000 of Dublin, but indisputably the largest town in the province of Ulster. There were those readers of the advertisement who would have known, some perhaps at first hand, of the cathedral-based 'meetings' in England which were later to be known as the Three Choirs festivals.[2] Some would have been aware also of the variety of festivals which had evolved in the midlands and the north of England, particularly those in Liverpool and Birmingham.[3] They would have known that towns which lacked choirs of their own could tie in to choral resources from neighbouring towns and churches, and engage soloists and instrumentalists from London; that there were expert, travelling festival conductors such as Dr Hayes of Oxford; that the Lancashire Trebles, an expert choral body of peripatetic ladies, had sung at the Three Choirs and at the Antient Concerts in London. It was good news that Bunting was going to mount a festival 'on a similar plan', but since Belfast was separated by the sea from the London resources of the English network, it would be using 'the first talents which this kingdom affords', which for practical purposes meant Dublin.[4] The newspapers honoured their pledge to 'communicate every information'; the degree of coverage given to the festival had not been seen since that accorded to the harpers, and it was not to be matched by another musical event for many years. The English festivals all had their origin in charity: the Belfast Charitable Society, a big charity with many initiatives, was known to

BELFAST

MUSICAL FESTIVAL.

FOR THE BENEFIT OF

THE INCORPORATED CHARITABLE SOCIETY.

UNDER THE PATRONAGE OF

MARQUIS OF DONEGALL,
MARCHIONESS OF DONEGALL,
MARQUIS OF DOWNSHIRE,
MARCHIONESS OF DOWNSHIRE,
COUNTESS OF CLANWILLIAM.
EARL OF MASSEREENE,
COUNTESS OF MASSEREENE,
EARL OF LONDONDERRY,
COUNTESS OF LONDONDERRY,
LORD VISCOUNT DUFFERIN,
LADY DUFFERIN,
LADY ELIZABETH PRATT,
LADY HARRIET FOSTER,
COLONEL FOSTER,
SIR EDWARD MAY, Bart.
LADY MAY,
SIR H. HERVEY BRUCE, Bart.
LADY BRUCE,
HON. R WARD,
LIEUTENANT-COLONEL FORDE,
GEORGE BRISTOW Esq. High Sheriff Co. Antrim,
THOMAS VERNER Esq. Sovereign of Belfast,
MRS. VERNER.
ALEXANDER STEWART Esq. Ards,
NICHOLAS PRICE Esq. Saintfield,
ROBERT BATESON Esq. Belvoir,
REV. DR. HUTCHESON Donaghadee,
REV. EDWARD MAY.
MRS MAY,
COLONEL HEYLAND,
MRS HEYLAND.
HUGH KENNEDY Esq. Cultra,
WILLIAM SHARMAN Esq Warringstown,
JOHN REILLY Esq. Scarva,
RICHARD DOBBS Esq. Castle Dobbs,
JAMES WATSON Esq. Brook Hill,
GEORGE DOUGLAS Esq. Mount Ida,
FRANCIS TURNLY Esq. Richmond Lodge,

STEWARDS.

The HIGH SHERIFF of the County of ANTRIM,
The SOVEREIGN of BELFAST,
LIEUTENANT-COLONEL COULSON,
REV MR. JEBB,
RICHARD DOBBS, ESQ.
ANDREW ALEXANDER, ESQ.
HENRY PURDON ESQ.

AT THE THEATRE,
ON TUESDAY EVENING, OCTOBER 19, 1813,
WILL BE PERFORMED,
A GRAND MISCELLANEOUS

CONCERT,

OF VOCAL & INSTRUMENTAL MUSIC.

AT DR. DUMMOND'S MEETING-HOUSE
On WEDNESDAY MORNING, OCT. 20,
A GRAND SELECTION OF

SACRED MUSIC,

From HANDEL, PURCELL, MARCELLO, &c.

AT SAME PLACE,
On THURSDAY MORNING OCT. 21,
HAYDN'S CELEBRATED ORATORIO OF

THE CREATION;

WITH A GRAND MISCELLANEOUS ACT,
SELECTED FOR THE OCCASION.

---

the THEATRE, on THURSDAY EVENING.

A MISCELLANEOUS CONCERT,

FROM THE WORKS OF
HAYDN, MOZART, AND BEETHOVEN.

AT DR. DRUMMOND'S MEETING-HOUSE,
ON FRIDAY MORNING, OCT. 22.
THE ORATORIO OF

THE MESSIAH,

PRINCIPAL VOCAL PERFORMERS.

Mrs. COOKE, Miss SPRAY,
Master ROBINSON, Master MULLEN,
Mr. SPRAY, Mr. JAGER, and
Mr. WEYMAN.

Leader of the Band ....Mr T. COOKE.
Second Violin ....Mr. BARRETT.
Tenor..............................Mr. BOWDEN.
Violincello......................Mr. BIRD
Double Bass....................Mr. SIDEBOTHAM.
Flute...............................Mr. WERDNER.
Oboe...............................Mr. B. COOKE.
Clarionet........................Mr. MAHON.
Bassoon ....Mr. BOND.
Horn...............................Mr. MULLIGAN.
Trumpet..........................Mr. WILMAN.
Trombone........................Mr. MEIGLER.
Double Drums...................Mr. GLOVER.

CONDUCTOR.........Mr. EDWARD BUNTING,
Who will preside at the Organ & Piano Forte.

The DEAN and CHAPTER of CHRIST'S CHRUCH, DUBLIN, having been pleased to grant permission for the principal part of the Choir to assist on this occasion, the CHORUSSES will be numerous and complete.—The entire Band will consist of above 50 Performers.

REGULATIONS.

Evening Concerts at the Theatre—The UPPER and LOWER BOXES, with an inclosed part of the PIT, are prepared for the accommodation of the Patrons, Patronesses, and other Subscribers of TWO GUINEAS.

[Of the Lower Boxes, Nos. 4, 5, 6, and 8, are kept for the Patrons and Patronesses.]

Plans of the Boxes, and Subscribers' part of the Pit, will be ready for inspection on MONDAY the 18th inst. at TWELVE o'Clock, at which hour places may be taken at the House of Mr. JOHN GALT SMITH, Secretary to the Committee, No. 26, High-street, to be entered in the exact order of application.

SINGLE TICKETS

For each of the EVENING CONCERTS, to the remaining parts of the House, will be ready for delivery as above, on Thursday next.

LETTICES, and Uninclosed part of the PIT, 10s. 10d.
GALLERY, ... 6s. 8d.
Single Tickets for each of the SACRED PERFORMANCES, in the Morning, at Dr. Drummond's Meeting-House, ... 12s. 6d.

N. B *All Tickets to be Transferable.*

Evening Concerts at the Theatre.—Doors to be opened at Seven o Clock, and the performance to commence precisely at Eight.

[Carriages to enter by Donegall-square and form a single line along Arthur-street, taking up in the same manner—Horses heads towards Corn-Market.]

Morning Sacred Performances, at Dr. Drummond's Meeting-House.—Doors to be opened at Eleven o'Clock, and commence precisely at Twelve.

[Carriages to enter by the Exchange, forming a single line along Rosemary street, taking up in the same manner—horses heads towards Hercules-street.]

To avoid confusion, no Money will be taken at the Doors for any of the performances, *nor Servants allowed to keep places*

Subscribers for the entire week's performance will be pleased to shew their Tickets to the Stewards—holders of Single Tickets to deliver theirs

After this Notice, it is expected that Subscribers will send for their Tickets without further delay.

☞ The Theatre lighted with Wax. (963

The advertisement of the festival in the *Belfast News-Letter*, 15 October 1813 the man in the street simply as 'the Poor-House'.

September was a good time for the festival, before the theatre seasons would have begun, but it proved over-optimistic. As the month began, the subscriptions were not coming in fast enough:

> the Conductor cannot subject himself to the risk of a heavy eventual loss in an attempt to bring forward an elegant entertainment of so high a description, without a previous certainty of sufficient funds.[5]

This seems to indicate that the festival was financed by subscriptions only; if so, at this late stage Bunting did not know how much he had to spend. The orders from the country were soon flooding in, however, for tickets and for places to stay; to a provincial town a festival could bring in a good deal of trade. At last it was confirmed that the festival would open on Tuesday 19th October:

> We understand that the entire band ... is to consist of about fifty performers: vocal sixteen, instrumental thirty-four. Among those already engaged, are Mrs Cooke, Miss Spray, Messrs Spray, Jager, Weyman &c, vocal. Principal instrumental performers: leader of the band, Mr T Cooke; second violin, Mr Barret; tenor [viola], Mr Robinson; violincello [*sic*], Mr Bird; double basses, Mr Sidebotham &c; flute, Mr Weidner; hautboy [oboe], Mr Metheringham; clarinet, Mr Mahon; horn, Mr Mulligan; bassoon, Mr Bond; trumpet, Mr Willman; trombone, Mr Millar; double drums, Mr Glover. Conductor, Mr Bunting, who will preside at the organ and pianoforte.[6]

The full advertisement, when it came, appeared less than a week before the first concert, by which time only single tickets were available for individual concerts. The patrons and stewards, headed by the marquis and marchioness of Donegall, are a fair spread of the nobility and gentry living in a compact, substantial territory comprising Belfast, the southern part of County Antrim, the northern part of County Down and part of eastern County Armagh. There is no sign of the hoped-for contribution from Newry and Derry. The events follow the English festival pattern of daytime performances of sacred music in a church alternating with evening concerts in a secular auditorium. Prices were high: a single ticket to a performance in the church would cost 12s 6d, to the theatre 10s 10d for the pit and 'lettices' (or lattices, the side galleries above the upper boxes), 6s 8d for the gallery; subscription tickets cost two guineas. The concerts in the theatre were to commence at eight o'clock, the performances in the church at noon. In anticipation of large attendances at the theatre, carriages were to come in by Donegall Square and form a line in Arthur Street with the horses' heads towards Cornmarket. For the church, they were to come in from the Exchange Rooms and form a line along Rosemary Street with the horses' heads towards Hercules Street (present-day Royal Avenue). No money would be taken at the doors, and servants would not be allowed to keep places. The theatre would be lighted with wax. The 'Conductor's Night' on Wednesday evening, Bunting's benefit, was separately advertised.[7]

The Exchange Rooms would have been the obvious choice to house the secular concerts, but the only occasion on which they were used in the entire festival was for the final ball and supper on the Friday night (also separately advertised), a charity event of great financial importance in some of the English festivals.[8] They were the only secular public rooms in the town, and booking them was extremely difficult: Bunting had managed to get them for his second Catalani visit in 1808, but for her first visit, in the previous year, he had had to take the theatre. In 1813 the theatre season fortunately did not begin until December. It was in the theatre that the two secular concerts and Bunting's benefit concert took place. It had a capacity of 700, but it was an unprepossessing place outside and chronically damp with a bad acoustic inside. For the sacred events (the term 'concert' was not used), St Anne's, where William Ware was still organist, was no doubt the expected venue. But the seven years since Bunting's move to Second Presbyterian had been the peak of his career: the culmination of his partnership with Dr Drummond was the festival, and the honour of housing Belfast's first *Messiah* fell to what is referred to in the advertisements and reports as Dr Drummond's Meeting-House.

A comparison of the list of performers with that given nine days earlier shows few changes. Master Robinson and Master Mullen are added to the vocal performers. Mr Robinson the viola player is replaced by Mr Bowden, Mr Metheringham the oboist by Mr B. Cooke; Mr Millar and Mr Meglier may well be the same man. For chorus (including vocal soloists), a formal request had been made to Christ Church Cathedral, and agreed to:

The Theatre, Arthur Street (now Arthur Square), Belfast, opened February 1793

PRIVATE COLLECTION

> The Marquis of Donegall requests use of some of the choir for a music festival in Belfast to benefit the Poor House, to be held in October ... if Mr Elliott [the master of the boys] would accompany them every possible care and attention should be paid to them ... [9]

Bunting's choral contact was in all probability Langrishe Doyle, his old teacher and still the organist of Christ Church. If the singing strength of the choir of Christ Church in 1813 was the same as that in the return made to the ecclesiastical commissioners in 1835 – six vicars choral, six stipendiaries and six choristers –[10] then it was indeed 'the principal part' which came north. Of the 'principal vocal performers', Master Robinson was Francis, the eldest of four brothers who were all to become leaders of the musical life of Dublin. Francis Robinson (who became Stanford's first harmony teacher)[11] was born in 1799; at Bunting's festival his career as a treble was nearing its end. John Spray had been a chorister at Southwell Minster and a lay-clerk at Lichfield before he came to Christ Church Cathedral, Dublin, as a tenor vicar choral in 1795. A difficult man, but much esteemed, a few weeks later he was to be given the freedom of Dublin.[12] Miss Spray was his daughter, with a good reputation in Dublin as a soprano.

Master Mullen's name does not occur in the reports of the events. Robert Jager, a lay clerk at Canterbury before coming to Christ Church as a stipendiary in 1810, could sing either counter-tenor or bass. David Weyman, a vicar choral in Christ Church and the bass soloist, was born in Dublin in 1771.[13] The only vocal soloist who was not a member of the choir of Christ Church was Mrs Cooke; an actress and singer, Fanny Howells to her maiden name, she was the wife of the leader of the band. Thomas Simpson Cooke, born in Dublin in 1782, was director of music in the Crow Street theatre. He had led the band when Bunting brought Catalani and her company to Belfast in 1807, obviously the instrumental contact Bunting needed. Cooke was a singer as well as an instrumentalist, and made a big enough success in Dublin in the tenor role of the Seraskier in Stephen Storace's opera *The Siege of Belgrade* to encourage him to cross the Irish Sea, where he sang the same part in London. Thereafter he had a busy career at Drury Lane and elsewhere in England for the rest of his life, as singer, violinist and composer of theatre music. His London début had taken place in July 1813. Luckily, he came back to Ireland to tidy up his affairs in the October; Bunting had got his man just in time.

The information given in the newspaper advertisements is supplemented by the list given in the programme for *Messiah* available to the audience[14] and by Bunting's list of fees.[15] The majority of performers are mentioned in both, but some who occur in one do not in the other. Of the thirty-odd instrumentalists, the majority can be identified as Dublin-based, mostly in Cooke's Crow Street theatre band. They include Bunting's brother Anthony, appearing as a cellist. Of the others, May, Giesler and Coleman can be identified as Belfast-based.[16] The fees of the Dublin players are, with very few exceptions, in double figures; seven of them receive 15 guineas apiece, and Cooke and Mrs Cooke have 100 between them. Of the local players, May and Coleman get 6 each, Giesler 3. The Sidebotham who plays the double bass does not get a fee; he may well be the Mr Sidebotham described in Bunting's list as the 'private secretary' who 'regulated every thing' and gets 30 guineas for that.[17] On a rough-and-ready separation, it seems reasonable to suppose that those who are down for 2 guineas are locally-based (McClean the oboe, Reed the bassoon,

Reilly the horn player, Maddison the trumpeter, Stokesbury the drummer) and may come, some of them, from the theatre and garrison bands.

Of the vocal soloists, there is Mrs Cooke's share of the 100 guineas; Jager and Weyman have 25 each, and Spray has 45 for himself and his daughter.[18] No fee is listed for Francis Robinson; this is presumably because he and the other Dublin cathedral choristers (none named) are to be recompensed within the 40 guineas paid to Mr Elliott. Some of the fees paid to the other chorus members are substantial. Broad, Duff and Blewitt have 30 guineas among them; Garbett, Webb and two illegibles 24; 'Gray and wife' 13, 'Barr and boy' 8. 'The chorusses' are said in the *Messiah* programme to be 'under the direction of Mr Blewitt'. Organist and theatre musician, he may have brought Broad and Duff with him from Dublin. Henry Barr is identifiable as having sung in the Bianchi/Haigh season in St Anne's; the 'boy' is perhaps his son. Two members of the Hart family which is deeply embedded in Belfast musical history receive 2½ guineas each, and so, as a chorus member, does another busy local musician, William Hughes. Several locally-based chorus members, such as the McCunes, senior and junior, appear, whether by choice or oversight, to receive no fee.

Both Barr and Hughes were Armagh-trained, and a direct Armagh contribution seems also to be evident. Four chorus members are described as 'Master' and receive no fee: they may be members of the choir of St Anne's or the Presbyterian churches, in which case one wonders what knowledge and experience they could have brought to singing *Messiah* in the daunting company of the Christ Church choristers. But if the 'Master Willis' is John Willis, future organist of St Anne's and major figure in the early choral society history of Belfast, then they may be from Armagh cathedral (Willis was Armagh-trained) and the expertise gap is narrowed. Mr Webb, who is Armagh-based and in receipt of a good fee, may well be the singer of the 1799 Bianchi-Haigh concerts in Belfast. The Garbett who appears with him in the fee list was often welcome from Armagh in Belfast concerts as John Garbett; the 'Garbutt' who appears in the *Messiah* programme as a violin in the band, but does not occur in the fee list, may be a misprint. It may be worth noting, at this early stage of the development of choral bodies in the British Isles (in which in the north of

England women played a considerable part) that the only women who appear in the two lists are Mrs Cooke and Miss Spray from Dublin, and the Mrs Gray who shares a chorus-member fee of 13 guineas with her husband in Bunting's list – all defined by the presence of their men.

When it was all over, the *Belfast News-Letter* of 22 October looked back on a summer of expectation and effort:

> From the day on which the Musical Festival was first suggested, the idea was eagerly embraced, and as the proposal combined rational amusement with the virtue of benevolence, it readily met the unqualified sanction of the public. Belfast had not before enjoyed the luxury of such a treat; and as the period approached, the public became more impatient, and nothing was talked of but the Festival, so that expectation was wound up to the highest pitch. The Committee and Stewards who undertook the charge of making the necessary arrangements, soon found that they had very arduous duties to perform; and on Mr. Bunting devolved the very important task of selecting and engaging the various professional gentlemen who were to compose the Band.

The opening concert in the theatre, with the performers placed on the stage in rising tiers of seats, was a social occasion.

> The Stewards, who who were distinguished by a red ribbon at their breast, and a white rod in their hand, took their respective stations ... In a little time, the two tiers of boxes, and the enclosed part of the pit, displayed as fine an assemblage of fashionable company as ever graced a theatre.[19]

The same edition of the *Belfast News-Letter* offered brief interim comment on the festival, praising the choruses and the Coronation Anthem. Tom Cooke and Mrs Cooke were commended, and so were Weyman, Spray and Jager, Weyman particularly for the first entry of the voice in *The Creation*, 'In the beginning God created the heavens and the earth' (the only mention of a specific number in the report of that oratorio). Miss Spray's effect was diminished by her diffidence. Willman's trumpet playing was highly praised. Of Bunting's performance 'it would be superfluous for us to speak'.

The *Belfast News-Letter* report of 26 October gave much more space to the festival, and occupied most of it with reproducing the programmes, in a few cases with the words of the songs. The festival had been attended by 'a much greater number of fashionable company than perhaps was ever assembled before in Belfast'. The *Messiah* performance was received with uncritical rapture; the 'Hallelujah' chorus had been encored. The trombones and trumpets were singled out for their effect in the choruses in both theatre and church. Bunting's organ playing got a special word, being 'so judiciously introduced and finely managed' and 'so delicately touched as to mingle its sounds almost imperceptibly'. Of the concerts in performance, the coverage was so thorough that it is possible to set out virtually the complete programmes performed (see Appendix 1). That of the first concert, in the theatre on Tuesday evening 19 October, had a good deal of music familiar to those who frequented concert room and theatre. The programme was light on the instrumental side, apart from Weidner's flute concerto. The sacred performance in the church on the following morning, Wednesday 20, was a mixture of the familiar and the less familiar: apart from Tom Cooke's violin concerto and Master Robinson's solo the music was entirely by Handel. Bunting's benefit that evening was not regarded as a festival concert, presumably to allow Bunting to retain the profits. It contained much home-grown music: an overture, a glee, a song and a trumpet concerto all by Cooke; a song, a glee and a duet by Stevenson. There were no less than three concertos, including Willman playing a trumpet concerto written for him by Cooke. Bunting played a piano concerto. But by whom? It is mentioned in two reviews.[20] The earlier, referring to the 'military concerto piano forte by Latour' (the terms in which it had been advertised), did so in the context of a criticism of the theatre's acoustic, saying 'it received great applause from the performers themselves, who were within hearing of it'. The other review referred to Bunting playing a concerto by Mozart, which 'produced the most delightful sensations on the few amateurs who were within hearing of it from the exquisitely light and delicate manner in which he executed it'. Even if one reviewer was unaware of a change of programme known to the other (and it can happen), and Bunting had, as seems the case, a light touch, the acoustic seems remarkably bad. It cannot be assumed that the audience were chattering; one of the reviewers specially mentions the attentive audience.[21]

In its report of Part One of the programme on the following morning, the *Belfast News-Letter* does not live up to its comprehensive standard, or perhaps was not given full information. Of *The Creation*, all the reader is given is the reviewer's appreciative reference to Weyman's singing. In the second half, Mrs Cooke's song, 'Hymn of Eve', is from Arne's first oratorio, *The Death of Abel*, written in Dublin and first performed there in 1744. The programme printed the words, as it did of some of the other pieces; no words were given of *The Creation*. The final secular concert took place that evening. Of the 'music by Haydn, Mozart and Beethoven' specified in the advertisement for this concert, there is only the Haydn symphony which opened the second half. A novelty was the concerto written by Cooke for Willman to play on the 'Kent bugle'.[22]

On the final day there came *Messiah* (See Appendix 1). Substantial omissions were accepted in *Messiah* performances, from Handel's own lifetime until relatively recently. Apart from 'And he shall purify', the Pastoral Symphony and 'He shall feed his flock', the omissions fall into three groups:

i the group containing

No 21, 'His yoke is easy'
No 22, 'Behold the Lamb of God'
No 24, 'Surely'
No 25, 'And with his stripes',

which is only broken by Jager singing No 23, 'He was despised';

ii the substantial group between 'Lift up your heads' and 'I know that my Redeemer liveth', containing

No 34, 'Unto which of the angels'
No 35, 'Let all the angels of God'
No 36, 'Thou art gone up on high'
No 37, 'The Lord gave the word'
No 38, 'How beautiful are the feet'
No 39, 'Their sound is gone out'
No 41, 'Let us break their bonds asunder'
No 42, 'He that dwelleth in heaven'
No 43, 'Thou shalt break them'

which is broken by Weyman singing No 40, 'Why do the nations', and the transference of No 44, 'Hallelujah' to end the oratorio, and

iii the group between 'The trumpet shall sound' and 'Worthy is the Lamb', containing

> No 49, 'Then shall be brought to pass'
> No 50, 'O death where is thy sting'
> No 51, 'But thanks be to God'.

It would be interesting to know if these omissions had become generally accepted in performance by 1813: six of them, asterisked in Appendix 1, together with No 52 'If God be for us', were frequently enough omitted to be relegated to an appendix of the Novello edition by Ebenezer Prout, ubiquitous in the nineteenth century, and not reinstated in their proper places until the revised Prout edition of 1942. A century after 1813, the practice of a newcomer to the musical scene in Belfast offers an interesting comparison. Edward Godfrey Brown came from Cumbria, studied violin, piano and organ at the Royal College of Music, and became a busy and prominent figure in the musical life of north-western England. When he came to Belfast in 1912 as conductor of the Belfast Philharmonic Society he circulated a pamphlet of 'simple directions for the chorus'.

BELFAST PHILHARMONIC SOCIETY.

HANDEL'S "MESSIAH."

Simple Directions for the Chorus.

BY

E. GODFREY BROWN

Please keep for future use.

The cover of Godfrey Brown's *Simple Directions for the Chorus*

Since it is dated December 1912, the choruses it covers are no doubt those of the performances he had been accustomed to conduct in England. These choruses do not include – because, it must be assumed, they were not part of his regular performance of *Messiah* –

> No 7, 'And he shall purify'

No 21, 'His yoke is easy'
No 25, 'And with his stripes'
No 35, 'Let all the angels of God'
No 37, 'The Lord gave the word'
No 39, 'Their sound is gone out'
No 41 'Let us break their bonds'
No 51, 'But thanks be to God'.

It is noteworthy that none of these was sung in the Bunting performance. The only other choruses which are covered in Godfrey Brown's pamphlet and were not sung in the Bunting performance are No 22, 'Behold the Lamb of God' and No 24, 'Surely'. The Prout appendix of usually-omitted solo numbers (Brown's pamphlet does not cover the solos) contained

No 34, 'Unto which of the angels'
No 36, 'Thou art gone up on high'
No 49, 'Then shall be brought to pass'
No 50, 'O death where is thy sting'
No 52, 'If God be for us'

all, be it noted, omitted in the Bunting performance except No 52. All the others are there, except for No 38, 'How beautiful are the feet', No 42, 'He that dwelleth in heaven' and No 43, 'Thou shalt break them'. On comparison, there appears a remarkable correspondence over almost a century; a 'complete' *Messiah* meant virtually the same in 1813 as it did in 1912. Indeed, Godfrey Brown's pamphlet was still in use at least until the outbreak of the second world war. He had been head of music in BBC Northern Ireland, so it may be presumed that he was well in touch with performing practice in the United Kingdom at large.[23] The interval break in the Bunting performance came after No 26, 'All we like sheep'. In the second part, No 53, 'Worthy is the Lamb', was followed by No 40, 'Why do the nations?', and No 44, 'Hallelujah', was the final chorus. These transferences do not occur in the Godfrey Brown version.

Bunting had Weyman for the bass solos, Spray for the tenor, and Jager, using his counter-tenor voice, for the alto. He had no less than three soprano soloists: Miss Spray, Mrs Cooke and the boy treble,

Francis Robinson. In the editorial attributions (see Appendix 1) it has been suggested that No 6, 'But who may abide', may have been by 1813 a bass aria, and that Master Robinson may have sung all four of the 'shepherds' numbers (Nos 14, 15, 16). There is an anomalous interlude, covering two numbers, the reasons for which do not appear in the sources. After Miss Spray's No 18, 'Rejoice greatly', Spray sings 'Come unto him' (the latter half of No 20). One would have expected one of the three sopranos to sing 'He shall feed his flock' (the first half of No 20, apparently omitted) and 'Come unto him' to be sung by Jager, not Spray. Mrs Cooke then sings an aria which is not from *Messiah* but *Jephtha*.

*

In the euphoria following the festival, the *Belfast News-Letter* report of 26 October had ended with a general compliment:

> Upon a retrospect of the whole of this first and splendid Musical Festival, we may pronounce, as the public opinion, that it was so judiciously arranged, so regularly conducted, and so charmingly performed, that we shall be glad to see its like again.

There is no doubt that Bunting's bold initiative had moved the concert life of Belfast substantially forward. Even in terms of organisation he had achieved what no-one else had achieved before him: every event advertised had taken place, and in substantially the terms advertised. The secular concerts had played the popular music of the day, a good deal of it familiar to the Belfast audience, but never so well performed. The reviewer who wished for a greater content of purely instrumental music may well have had in mind the considerable riches of the concerto and symphony repertoire. By 1813 Mozart and Haydn had bequeathed the totality of their enormous legacy; Beethoven had written eight of his nine symphonies, the violin concerto and all of his piano concertos. If the promise of music from the works of Haydn, Mozart and Beethoven in the advertisement of the Thursday evening concert had proved over optimistic, the same did not apply to the vocal content. Fortunately, Handel's stature as a composer had, then as now, been uniquely matched by his universal popularity. With all due acknowledgment of the variety and professionalism of the whole festival, its great achievement was the bringing to Belfast for the first time of *Messiah*, the greatest work of a major composer. It was Bunting's achievement, the credit not to be denied him.

NOTES

1 *BN-L*, and *BCC*, 7, 8 May 1813.
2 The Three Choirs festival was, and still is, based on the cathedrals of Gloucester, Hereford and Worcester.
3 For the development, see BRIAN PRITCHARD, *The musical festival and the choral society in England in the 18th and 19th centuries: a social history* (unpublished PhD thesis, Birmingham, 1966); and WILLIAM WEBER, *The rise of musical classics in 18th-century England: a study in canon, ritual and ideology* (Oxford, Clarendon Press, 1992).
4 Ireland continued to be referred to as 'this kingdom', despite the Act of Union of 1800.
5 *BCC*, 4 September 1813.
6 *BCC*, 6 October 1813.
7 *BN-L*, 15, 19 October 1813.
8 *BN-L*, 15 October 1813.
9 *Christ Church Chapter Acts, September 1809 – January 1818* (Representative Church Body, C/6/1/7/9, 208). I am grateful to Dr Barra Boydell for this information. The request from Belfast made no mention of the venue being a Dissenting church; Dr Boydell suggests that the charity aspect would no doubt have ensured consent in any case.
10 GRINDLE, *Irish cathedral music*, p. 61.
11 RICHARD PINE and CHARLES ACTON (eds), *To talent alone: the Royal Irish Academy of Music 1848–1998* (Dublin, Gill and Macmillan, 1998), p. 404.
12 *BN-L*, 25 January 1814.
13 He was not unknown in Belfast; he was the author of *Melodia Sacra*, available in the local shops (*BCC*, 9 May 1812), a collection of settings of the Psalms which was widely used in Irish parish churches before the appearance in 1864 of the first edition of the Irish Church Hymnal.
14 1900 typescript of Book of Words from the 1813 *Messiah* performance belonging to Miss Jane Dunn (sister of John Dunn, secretary of the Classical Harmonists' Society). The original Book of Words was presented to the Belfast Philharmonic Society: information from David Byers' website: www.btinternet.com/~david.byers/homepage.htm.
15 'Account of Money paid performers, and to be paid, at the Music Festival, Belfast': *Bunting* MSS, 4/26/48. The document is dated 24 October 1813. Obviously written down in a hurry, it has its crossings-out and illegibilities, but is *faute de mieux* an invaluable document.
16 Coleman has appeared in this esssay as playing with Bunting in one of the Bianchi/Haigh concerts in 1799, Giesler in a concert with Bunting, Haigh, Byrne and Coleman in 1802. Several musicians called May occur in the musical life of Belfast; this could be the James (?) May who led the band in the theatre at this time. James Thompson May, who became a force in Belfast music for many years, is not for certain found in the sources earlier than 1835.
17 Mr J. Galt Smith appears in the publicity as secretary of the festival. No doubt

a good deal of the routine work devolved on an assistant.

18 On the reverse side of the page listing the fees, Bunting has written, 'Paid Spray out of my own pocket 5 guineas, as he said that his rank as first tenor deserved it'.

19 *BN-L*, 22 October 1813.

20 *BN-L*, 22, 26 October 1813.

21 Professor Donald Burrows has suggested that Bunting's piano may have been a square, which would help to account for the small tone. The square piano had by no means vanished from the Belfast scene. William Ware had for sale in *BN-L*, 20 July 1802, a 'new square piano forte, with additional keys and Grasshopper Touch, from Dublin'. Six years after Bunting's festival he had two squares for sale in *BN-L*, 9 April 1819. Broadwood did not discontinue the manufacture of squares until 1860: EHRLICH, *Piano*, p. 48.

22 A bandmaster had added keys to the common military bugle in Dublin in 1810; it was a popular instrument for some years until it was superseded by the valved instruments.

23 When Godfrey Brown became director of music in the BBC in Belfast in 1924, he compiled an exhaustive list of orchestral works with their instrumentation and timings. Sir John Reith wrote to thank and congratulate him; it was a monumental work, he said, which would be extremely useful to the BBC all over the country. It remained in use even after being superseded by more up-to-date reference books: MALCOLM RUTHVEN, *Belfast Philharmonic Society 1874–1974: a short history* (Belfast, 1974), p. 32.

8
FALL FROM GRACE

BY THE MIDDLE OF THE SECOND DECADE of the nineteenth century Edward Bunting had produced two volumes of a collection of Irish traditional music which in scale and thoroughness was without precedent. In mainstream music, admiration of him as a keyboard executant had been expressed by visiting professionals. In Belfast he was the organist of one of its churches, leading the music on an instrument he had helped to design. He taught music in school and took private pupils. He had promoted subscription concerts, and visits in two successive years by Catalani. He had been the musical director of a festival which had brought *Messiah* in full and *The Creation* in part to Belfast for the first time. The example of his work on the ancient music had brought into being the Irish Harp Society and its school. With the return of peace in Europe and the increase in the town's population there was a substantial audience to welcome systematised concert promotion. The festival had set up the possibility of regular oratorio festivals on the British model. The ancient music awaited its final definitive volume at Bunting's hands. Yet of these three areas of activity only the last-named was to receive his continuing attention, and that at a much reduced work rate.

Now in his early forties, the tide of initiative had ebbed. Like Ware before him and many after him, he was disposed to forsake the marketplace for the elevated security of the organ loft. It was one element of a perceptible process in which Bunting withdrew (or was withdrawn?) from the central position he had established in the musical life of Belfast. For if he was no longer inclined to put forward fresh projects on his own initiative, it has to be said that external stimuli from his fellow-townspeople were also lacking. There is no expression in the public prints of a wish to have Bunting reinstate the subscription concert series of which he had now so much experience. If perhaps Bunting himself had said goodbye to that activity and was not to be moved, he could have had his reasons. The only secular auditoria in the town large enough for concerts were the Exchange Rooms and the theatre. So great were the demands of the ever-growing business community that a new and bigger exchange was in contemplation, to be opened in 1820 as the Commercial Buildings (still extant in Waring Street); in the meantime the over-used and ageing Exchange Rooms were almost impossible to book. The theatre, never a good concert auditorium, was now suffering from the social blight that was to affect the theatre in general for a good part of the nineteenth century. If Bunting had decided that he had had enough of the stresses and uncertainties of concert promotion, he was, it seems, by no means alone. It was a time when the middle classes, the concert audiences of the future, were greatly increasing in numbers, and the era of the touring celebrity was at hand. Catalani had been to Belfast already, invited by Bunting, and the next three decades would see the visits of Kalkbrenner, the Herrmann Quartet and Paganini, all on their own initiative – yet nobody else in Belfast, for many years, was prepared to promote such virtuosi, much less undertake subscription series.

As the festival ended the *BN-L* reviewer had looked forward to 'its like'. Circumstances militated against repeat festivals in the two years immediately following. In August 1814 there seemed a good opportunity. There was a peace festival in Dublin. It was premature – Napoleon escaped from Elba and the bonfires all over Europe had to be lit again after Waterloo – but it took place on a metropolitan scale. It used St Werburgh's church (the parish church of Dublin Castle) and the Rotunda. The entire band numbered more than one hundred,[1] and the augmented chorus included the Lancashire Trebles. Catalani sang 'Comfort ye' and 'Every valley' as well as the soprano solos. Could Catalani have been captured for a Belfast festival while she was in Ireland? Even if she could have been, it was too soon; for everybody involved in Belfast, the effort of running the 1813 festival made at least one fallow year necessary before tackling it again. 1815, a year further on, offered surely a better prospect; the fallow year over, the real peace to be celebrated. But the times were unpropitious. Bunting's network of contacts had disintegrated. Langrishe Doyle had retired from Christ Church; Tom Cooke had gone to London; Dr Drummond had accepted a call to a church in Dublin. There were in any case many substantial obstacles in the way of establishing a custom of annual or regular sacred-and-secular festivals. There was no provincial festival structure in Ireland. In any attempt to emulate the English system, the logistics of an Irish provincial-town festival were much more formidable. The road system in England had helped the Three Choirs festivals to draw on both neighbouring and London-based resources, and the roads which the industrial revolution brought into being helped the development of the midlands and northern festivals later. The Irish Sea was a barrier of a quite different and much more expensive sort. Bunting's admirable initiative had fallen on too stony a ground. An important adverse circumstance in Belfast itself was that there was as yet no choral impetus. In England the northern and midlands choral societies grew out of the festival movement, a seamless evolution showing the sacred-and-secular format to have been a transitional model. Choral societies were to proliferate in Belfast, but not until the 1840s and 1850s, and owing nothing to Bunting's example. They came into being, not within the context of the concert life of the town, but because of the concern of the churches to improve their congregational singing. It was 1856 before the next complete *Messiah*. It had its own chorus, its own string orchestra, and at the organ the organist of Armagh cathedral. The soloists came from Dublin, Armagh and Hillsborough, and for imported celebrity there was Charles Lockey, who had been the tenor soloist at the first performance of Mendelssohn's *Elijah* at Birmingham a few years earlier. Five years had gone into the preparation of the performance on this model; but it immediately became the annual event which it has remained.

The 1813 festival was enthusiastically advertised in advance and reported in unprecedented detail during its course. The novelty and quality of so much of the music, especially *Messiah*, the orchestral and vocal content of the concerts, the quality of the performers – in all these Bunting was given his full meed of praise. But some four weeks after the festival ended there appeared in the press a brief financial summary.[2] The 'total amount of tickets issued' had come to £1,207 4s 11d. 'General expenditure' was £945 0s 3½d. The net amount for the benefit of the Belfast Poor House was £262 4s 7½d, a paltry sum in comparison with the cross-channel festivals.[3] By far the largest item in the general expenditure had been the £638 paid by Bunting in fees to the performers.

A few days later the *Belfast News-Letter* printed the first of two substantial instalments of its 'Critical Remarks on the late Musical Festival in Belfast, written on the probability of its being occasionally repeated' (reproduced as Appendix 2)[4]. It was unsigned, the writer someone of knowledge, some breadth of experience, and mature judgment.[5] A critical notice of a performance either in concert room or theatre was very rare at this date; one of this length was quite exceptional, and poses questions as to why it was written, and at this relatively late juncture.

After two introductory paragraphs on 'oratorio', the festival is acknowledged by the writer to have been a success (para. 3), notwithstanding 'very prescribed means' – a warning shot of a broadside to come later. In the 'observations on the performances', the acoustic of the theatre is roundly criticised and deficiencies of the vocal items laid to its charge; more instrumental (i.e. non-vocal) music would have improved the programmes, 'the band being powerful, harmonious and complete' (paras 4–7). In the 'morning performances', the church as an auditorium incurs no criticism, and offers 'the aid of a very fine organ, touched by the masterly hand of Mr Bunting' (para. 8). The content of the first performance receives detailed and appreciative treatment, unlike the brief notes on the secular concerts. Unstinted praise is not to be the order of the day, however. Haydn's *Creation* comes in for serious criticism as a work, comparison with Handel redounding not at all to its credit (paras 11–12).[6] It is by no means an uninformed criticism: the appreciation of Haydn as a composer of orchestral music which follows is authoritative enough. With a comparison of 'simple airs' with 'execution', to the latter's detriment, the author shows himself a man of his time; it was a favourite opposition. There, the first of the two instalments ends – except for a note (the placing surely deliberate) on how much less 'prescribed' the financial means had been for a recent festival in England:

> The late Liverpool Festival produced, by a *Sermon*, with which it opened, £300 – *Tickets* for its five performances produced £4,500 – A Ball, £1,250 and a donation from one of its Members of Parliament, £50, making an aggregate of *£6,050!*, near one-third of which went to charitable funds. The number of Subscribers was 1,250. Persons at one time in the ballroom, 2,228 (para. 13).

No doubt some readers recalled the announcement in another newspaper on the euphoric eve of the Belfast festival, that at the Three Choirs Festival in Hereford, *Acis and Galatea* and *Messiah* had been performed to an audience of 800 and the total collection at the church doors, 'with donations since received', had totalled £614.[7]

Having kept his most telling comment on the organisation of the festival to a footnote of his first instalment, the writer of the critique commences his second with the extended eulogy of the *Messiah* performance which the unique quality of the event demands and which his still basking readership expects. The heights of his praise of Handel and his masterpiece are reached with an extended quotation from *Paradise Lost* (para. 16). Leaving his readers with the conviction that nothing should be too good for the next Belfast performances of the greatest music in the world, he then (para. 17) embarks, by a deadly comparison, on an exposé of the many places where the recent festival fell short of that lofty goal. Since cathedrals are 'most appropriate to such entertainments', the parish church of Belfast, *with its organ in good order* (emphasis added)[8] would be preferable to 'other places of worship'. The festival might then commence with a sermon by a dignitary of the establishment, for the sole benefit of the poor, 'the propriety of which may be estimated by the collection on a similar occasion at Liverpool'. A Dissenting church is, by implication, no substitute (para. 18).[9] Whatever circumstances may have dictated the dates of Bunting's festival, a future festival should take place

> either immediately on the breaking up of the great musical meetings in England, or on the occasional visits of the best singers to our Irish metropolis. On such occasions, one or two of the first rate singers that our sister country affords might be procured on moderate terms (para. 19).

The logic is irrefutable, addressing as it does the advantages enjoyed by the English festivals and by Dublin, the Irish metropolis, in attracting the best talent. The final sentence of the paragraph, 'The value even of ONE supereminent voice, and the beneficial effect it would have on the receipts, are obvious', implies that no such voice graced the Belfast festival, *pace* Mrs Cooke.[10] Paragraph 20 puts the basic concept of a festival in its place. The charity aspect must take precedence. Thrift is essential, followed by 'least trouble to the Inhabitants' (whatever in retrospect that may have meant).

Then the writer makes his central, radical, suggestion:

> ... a single individual should take future festivals at his own risque, with an ultimate view of deriving profit from them... one person would have an interest in carrying it into effect in the best manner, securing such vocal and instrumental performers as would ensure him success ... and studying a prudent economy in every thing (para 20).

To help digestion there are further suggestions. The chief singers and principal instrumental performers should be announced before any tickets are issued, at least a month preceding it, 'in order that the entertainment to be expected may be early ascertained' (para. 21). For the theatre there should be substituted the Exchange Rooms 'with the addition, if found requisite, of the two smaller rooms ... 300 auditors could ... be accommodated with perfect convenience' (para 22).[11] Paragraphs 23 and 24 repeat the plea for more instrumental music and raise the question of precedence seating, presumably because like other aspects, some noted, some not, it had caused annoyance.[12]

With a criticism of 'the glees at supper' (para. 26), the writer signs off, and then, as with his first instalment, discharges a Parthian shaft. A very serious one, reserved to the last, and introduced by a pointing finger for emphasis:

> In England, Dignitaries of the Church encouraged the performance of Oratorios. Not one Reverend Bishop graced the Festival at Belfast (para. 27).

It is not quite the end of the critique – Bunting is praised for his playing of a Corelli concerto in the *Messiah* performance (para. 28) – but the damage has been done. The shortcomings in the planning and organisation of the festival have been comprehensively enumerated. Of those responsible none can escape the censure, however gently administered and with whatever recognition of the achievement. In the proposal of a businessman to assume command of future festivals, the writer had presumably in mind someone like Joseph Moore. Festivals had taken place in Birmingham since the 1750s, but there had been a great leap forward in their efficient and profitable running and, be it said, imaginative programming, since Joseph Moore, a businessman, had taken over in 1799.[13] As with many a purveyor of radical advice, the writer of the critique offers no solutions to the obvious problems – the Exchange Rooms, St Anne's and its organ, the finding of a Belfast counterpart to Joseph Moore (no other English festival had found one either). The most deadly point, for the purposes of this essay, is that Edward Bunting is not even named as assisting with the artistic content of future festivals, let alone retaining the responsibility for running it. Bunting is side-lined. He may, like Ware before him, have decided that he had had enough of concert promotion; but, taken with the disclosure of the financial out-turn, the critique left him with little choice.

If this interpretation of the critique seems hypothetical, there is a subsequent development in the musical life of Belfast which lends it credence. Late in the 1814–15 season a violinist, Mlle Gerbini, advertised her second concert in the Exchange Rooms as 'by particular desire of the Marquis of Donegall, Thomas Verner Esq, Sovereign, and of the President and Members of the Anacreontic Society'.[14] A private music club had come into existence, its formation not noticed in the newspapers.[15] By the spring of 1816 it had been long enough in existence to attract attention, appreciative and admonitory, in the pages of a journal:

> These reflections were strongly created in my breast a few evenings ago, when passing by our Exchange, I heard the sweet and melodious sounds of a well-regulated band of music … I stopped and listened, when memory whispered that this was a regular night of meeting of the 'Anacreontic Society'… This society (I understand) has existed several years, and has, under the tuition and auspices of a most accomplished, scientific, experienced leader, arisen to great perfection in this ingenious and delightful, but difficult art. Their numbers are very considerable, and they meet at stated periods …[16]

The writer ended with a plea to the society to aid the cause of charity, which was heeded in the following season. In the advertisement of a concert for the benefit of the House of Industry on 10 February 1817 the band of the society was mentioned as performing.[17] In the newspaper report the names were given of the society's officers and directors, including the leader, who had been referred to in the *Belfast Literary Journal* in terms reminiscent of those applied to Bunting a few years earlier:

Marquis of Donegall, President. Thomas Verner Esq, Vice-President
Mr Guerini, Leader of the Band Mr W Sloane, Secretary
Lt Col Coulson Dr Thomson Capt Daniel Mr Ross
Mr Bradshaw Mr George Joy Mr John Bunting Mr Wm Cairns

Vincenzo Guerini had taken up residence in town in 1806, describing himself as a native of Italy and offering to teach Italian, pianoforte and singing, 'with the advantage of accompanying on the violin'.[18] The programme included a piano concerto by Dussek, played in 'a clear, correct and chaste manner' by John Bunting. Not only was Edward Bunting not the leader of the society's band, but their piano soloist was his brother. In 1796 John Bunting had been living in Newry. In 1804 his wife was advertising her school in Belfast as an established enterprise,[19] so he may be presumed to be living in Belfast from that time at least; his name is met with for another few years in the Anacreontic Society and in St Anne's.[20] But it was his brother Edward who had had the established reputation in Belfast as a keyboard soloist for a long period of years; he was still an active organist, and one cannot imagine that he would not have played a piano concerto if asked. The repudiation of Edward Bunting by the Anacreontic Society falls into place in the context of the hypothesis.

*

Edward Bunting was now in his forties, and in appearance the comfortable figure of the Brocas portrait. In 1815 he had travelled in Europe and had met musicians in France and Belgium, played Irish airs to them and played on organs in Antwerp and Haarlem. In Paris his appearance, so obviously that of the portly English gentleman,

Edward Bunting in his late thirties, from the portrait of 1811
by the young William Brocas, 1794–1868

NATIONAL GALLERY OF IRELAND

had caused derisive cries of 'Jean Bull!'[21] But his initiatives had not been unmixed with disappointment. The success of his work on the 'ancient music' had been soured by the popularity of Moore's Melodies. Financially, he had made very little money from his two collections, which had been quickly pirated in Dublin. Of his harper friends the two most eminent, Denis Hempson and Arthur O'Neill, had died in 1807 and 1816 respectively.

He was also no longer at ease in Second Presbyterian. In the early days, £50 had been 'voted to Mr Bunting … and thanks for his very great attention since the introduction of the organ, £50 for performing thereon, and £40 annually from 1st May'. The congregation regretted 'that they cannot pay more for his very great ability'.[22] By 1814, however, a dispute had arisen which was not resolved until two years later when 'a letter from Mr Bunting was read accepting £60 per year for the conducting of Musick'.[23] Mutual dissatisfaction was soon to reach a head. In 1811 the rebuilding of the old corporation church at the foot of High Street, dismantled at the time of the erection of St Anne's forty years earlier, had commenced, and in late 1816 Second Presbyterian granted St George's (the name by which the new church was to be known) the use of their church while the interior was being completed.[24] The St George's parishioners had the pleasure of having Bunting play for their services as well as those of his employers. Bunting on his part was feeling the strain of separation from the anglican tradition, especially now that his friend and encourager Dr Drummond had left Second Presbyterian. In June 1817 the church committee had before it a substantial report from the sub-committee appointed 'to enquire respecting the Musical department'.[25] The management of the Poor House boys was unsatisfactory:[26] they were not 'accompanied by the organ when practising', and it was suggested that the organist as part of his duties should devote '1 day per week for 1 or 2 hours to practise with the children'. It was recommended that 'a sub-committee of 2 or 3 should superintend and direct if necessary the musical department'. Having heard

> that Mr Bunting had made, or was about to make, an engagement to play the organ in the Chapel of Ease [St George's], they thought it right to make enquiry respecting the fact, from which they find Mr Bunting had made such engagement and entered upon the duty of it 2 months ago.

Bunting was reprimanded for playing 'symphonies' between the verses of the psalms. 'Symphonies', or interludes between the vocal sections of anthems or the verses of psalms and hymns, were a well-established feature of parish church music.[27] In some of the tunes in his *Sacred Harmony* William Ware includes 'symphonies'; some are two bars long, none longer than four. They may be intended to be

A 'symphony' from Ware's *Sacred Harmony*

played as written, or, in the hands of an able organist, a basis of improvisation (for Bunting one would imagine the latter). They are referred to as 'essential to the Performance' by Ware in his advertisement of the publication of *Sacred Harmony*. Bunting had no doubt been accustomed to playing them in Second Presbyterian, to the delight of Dr Drummond; but from a sterner presbyterianism the ground of the reprimand was that

> they break in too much upon the solemnity of the devotion of that part of our service by leading the mind to consider the fine-ness of the music more than the praise of God.

Receiving the report, the church stopped short of dismissing their once distinguished employee, and decided that

> Mr Bunting is to be informed of regulations adopted respecting the

> music and asked whether the congregation can expect his conformity thereto, and his regular services hereafter as organist or not.

His exit was complete by the end of the summer:

> The Chairman had written to Bunting as above but had not as yet received any answer' (Meeting of 6 July1817).
>
> The Chairman was requested to write to Bunting that as no answer has been received to the letter addressed to him on 5 June last the committee considers he has resigned the situation of organist in this house, and request that he may furnish his account (Meeting of 3 August 1817).
>
> Resolved that from henceforth Mr Bunting shall not be continued as organist of this house … that this be communicated to Mr Bunting and the key of the organ required from him (Meeting of 7 September 1817).

Bunting had become the first organist of St George's.

NOTES

1 *FDJ*, 9 August 1814.
2 *BCC*, 17 November 1813.
3 The final sum received by the Charitable Society was £259 13s 8d: *BCC*, 19 January 1814.
4 *BN-L*, 20, 23 November 1813.
5 A later hand has written 'by H. Joy' at the head of the first instalment in the copy held in the Linen Hall Library. No corroboration has so far been possible, but the attribution may not be unreasonable.
6 It was not an unusual judgment for its time. The opinion was quickly formed that *The Creation* was inferior to Handel's oratorios; as early as 1802 it became usual to perform only the first part of the work in England, culminating in 'The heavens are telling': NICHOLAS TEMPERLEY, *Haydn: The Creation* (Cambridge Music Handbooks, Cambridge University Press, 1991), p. 40. The Belfast performance may have been of the first part only.
7 *BCC*, 18 October 1813.
8 If the organ, installed some thirty years earlier, was in need of renovation, this might have been an additional reason for Bunting to place his festival elsewhere.
9 The writer has conveniently forgotten the charity sermon preached in Second Presbyterian seven years earlier which yielded £214 5s 6d: *BCC*, 1 December 1806.
10 The Dublin *Monthly Panorama* in February 1810 had damned her with faint praise: 'she has a sweet, melodious, and without any pretensions to excel in the higher range of her profession, a cultivated and well-managed voice … there is a naiveté and beauty and infantine delicacy in the tones that are equally attractive': quoted in WALSH, *Opera in Dublin 1798–1820*, p. 126.
11 Surely an exaggerated claim; amenity apart (and it was a beautiful auditorium) the large room, 60 feet by 30, would have difficulty in accommodating this size of audience, especially with so many singers and players, with their instruments and piano. Its attraction, however, to the social sector who needed to be attracted was undeniable in comparison with the theatre.
12 The two aspects are not unrelated; in Belfast at least, on the evidence of such socially conscious bodies as the Belfast Musical Society of the previous century, the higher echelons of society preferred instrumental music.
13 His business was in die-sinking (engraving of dies) and button-making: PRITCHARD, p. 231.
14 *BN-L*, 3 March 1815.
15 The date of its formation is to be deduced retrospectively; as a random example from many, the concerts of 1855–6 are described in the advertisements as 'forty-second season'.
16 *Belfast Literary Journal*, April 1816, pp. 35–7, signed 'Orpheus'.
17 *BN-L*, 28 January 1817.
18 *BN-L*, 8 August 1806.

19 *BN-L*, 17 January 1804.

20 When St Anne's advertised in 1817 for three persons to assist in vocal music, application was to be made to 'Rev Brown, Mr Ware or Mr John Bunting': *BN-L*, 5 December 1817.

21 PETRIE, *Bunting*, p. 71.

22 *Minutes of Second Presbyterian Church* (held in the Public Record Office of Northern Ireland), meeting of 10 April 1808.

23 *Minutes*, meeting (undated), 1816.

24 S. SHANNON MILLIN, *History of the Second Congregation of Presbyterian Dissenters in Belfast* (Belfast, Baird, 1900), p. 105.

25 *Minutes*, meeting of 1 June 1817.

26 In 1812 four boys from the Poor House had been 'bound to the organist in trust for the congregation' for a number of years: *Minutes*, meeting of 13 May 1812.

27 See TEMPERLEY, *English parish church*, vol. 1, p. 199.

9
EPILOGUE

IN THE YEARS SINCE THE 1799 CONCERTS, in which both Ware and Bunting took part and were specially thanked by the visiting professionals, relations between the two men had not been severed, as is shown by their sharing of the organ at a charity sermon in St Anne's in 1816 while Bunting was still the organist of Second Presbyterian.[1] In the new century, Ware went on selling pianos into the 1820s. He did not confine his activities, however, to the organ of St Anne's, his wife's school and the selling and servicing of pianos. In 1802, while Bunting was still in St Anne's, the author of a first volume and heavily engaged in the research for a second, Ware had ventured on authorship himself:

> SACRED MUSIC
>
> William Ware, Organist of Belfast Church, having prepared a Selection of the several PSALMS, HYMNS and ANTHEMS performed in that Church, with the addition of many others meant to be introduced and performed occasionally; intends publishing the whole in one large folio Volume, elegantly engraved and printed on the best Paper – Price to Subscribers, One Guinea, to be paid on delivery of the Work, which is now in the hands of the Engraver, and will be ready in the month of June next.

Subscriptions were to be received by Ware himself, by three Belfast music sellers, the organists of Hillsborough and Armagh, and all the music shops in Dublin. The work would contain a list of the subscribers 'to distinguish the Encouragers of the undertaking'. He had also exerted his utmost endeavours, aided by the experience of many years,

> to render the above Work interesting, as well to the attendants on the

> Service of the Church, as to private families who possess the advantage of an Harpsichord or Piano Forte; the arrangement being made so as to render the Voice part simple and intelligible, and the Instrumental part, Treble and Bass, full and accordant, including the Symphonies and Interludes essential to the Performance; whilst at the same time, due regard is paid to that simplicity of expression, which in Sacred Music is so peculiarly desirable.[2]

Far from being ready in a few months, and despite the author's appeal to the wider market, the book took nearly seven years to reach publication. It was November 1808 before Ware was able to express the hope that 'it will be ready for delivery next month, one half of the Plates being already engraved',[3] and ten months later before its arrival in the shops, dedicated to the marchioness of Donegall, was announced (for the frontispiece see page 12).[4] It made its appearance a month after the advance notice of Bunting's second collection.[5] The list of subscribers, while commendably lengthy, lacked the range of eminent names which had appeared in Michael Thomson's anthems a generation earlier; the Donegall family had nothing like the political and ecclesiastical influence of the Downshires.

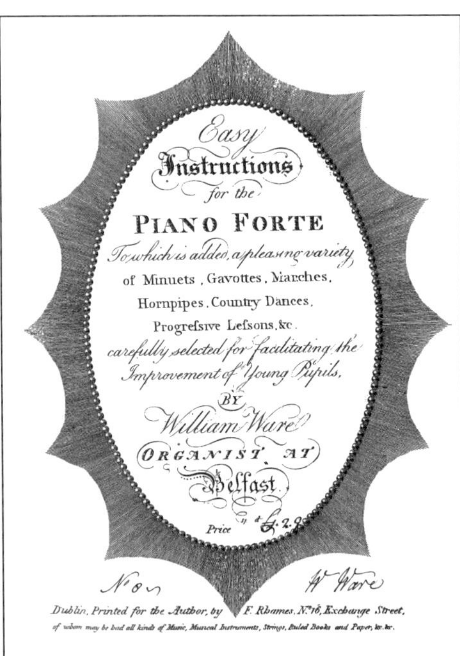

Easy
Instructions
for the
PIANO FORTE
To which is added, a pleasing variety
of Minuets, Gavottes, Marches,
Hornpipes, Country Dances,
Progrefsive Lefsons, &c.
carefully selected for facilitating the
Improvement of Young Pupils,
BY
William Ware
ORGANIST AT
Belfast.
Price
Dublin, Printed for the Author, by F. Rhames, N° 16, Exchange Street,
of whom may be had all kinds of Music, Musical Instruments, Strings, Ruled Books and Paper, &c. &c.

The frontispiece of Ware's *Easy Instructions*, from the copy held in the Linen Hall Library

It was not Ware's only book. At the time of the original announcement of his church music book, he had another on the stocks. In the following year, aiming at a different but not unrelated market, he announced the publication of his *Easy Instructions for the Piano Forte*.[6] Ware was exploiting the piano boom, with foresight and accuracy. While *Sacred Harmony* was working through its long gestation, *Easy Instructions* ran to a second edition,[7] and what looks like a third came out three years later.[8]

Ware died in 1826 at the age of sixty-nine. His talent for being up with or ahead of the market never deserted him, as a spectacular instance shows in his late fifties. Johann Bernhard Logier, proprietor of a music business in Dublin, invented a mechanism for training pianists, a laterally sliding frame for the hands fitted above the keyboard. He called it 'the chiroplast' and patented it in 1814. It did not reach London until 1817, but Ware had it, transported and set up in his own house, within a year of its patenting:

NEW SYSTEM OF MUSICAL EDUCATION.

MR WARE

> Most respectfully informs the Nobility, Gentry and his Friends in general, that from the astonishing improvement made in the SCIENCE OF TEACHING MUSIC by Mr J.B. LOGIER of Dublin, he has procured one of his newly invented Apparatus for facilitating the acquirement of a proper execution on the Piano Forte, with every necessary Book of Instruction, and approves of it so much, that in future he intends adopting it with such new Pupils as he may be honoured with. Any Lady or Gentleman may see the Apparatus by calling at his house in Great Edward Street.
>
> P.S. Mr WARE has not the smallest doubt of succeeding on this plan, and although some Professional Gentlemen differ with him, yet there is every probability of a Child being more readily grounded in the first Rudiments of Music in *Six Months*, than in *Twelve* by the old method.[9]

Ware's researches and publishing initiatives were independent of Edward Bunting's; in neither man's books is there a reference to the other. In a letter of 1809 to Mary Ann McCracken, Bunting, feeling greatly hurt at that time at what he saw as the unacknowledged pillaging of his first volume by Thomas Moore and the Power brothers, referred to Ware as 'that old fool'.[10] As has been seen, there was no permanent rift between them. They had gone their separate ways, Ware on a more conventional career. No doubt Bunting's annoyance, as expressed to Mary Ann McCracken, rested on his conviction that he had left Ware behind, that he had learnt all that Ware could teach him. In expertise on organ and piano, and on promotion of concerts, he had. But there were skills which, to his cost, he had not learnt from Ware. Ware had had his successful enterprises, and his failures. He knew how to spot the opening and to exploit the market; he also knew how, when an initiative was unproductive, to withdraw before suffering undue damage, and to cover his losses within his proven enterprises. He ran his career astutely, and he made a very good living at it. He had also long realised that he would spend his life in the town he now lived in. He knew that the cathedrals of Armagh and Dublin were not open to his abilities as an organist, and that in his various business enterprises he would prosper no better in any other Irish town than the rapidly expanding Belfast; a typically rational decision. Possibly the financial and other disappointments in Bunting's career could not have been avoided. But one cannot help feeling that, had he recognised the value of observing William Ware in some of the other fields in which Ware was a master, it would have benefitted him.

Bunting was no doubt hurt by his post-festival repudiation by the Belfast musical public at large, but he lacked Ware's capacity for counting his blessings. As an organist he had returned to the anglican tradition in which he had been reared, potentially revitalised with a new post and a new organ in a new church. His two collections had set up the urgent need for the final, definitive, third which he of all people was the man to produce. In early middle age he had slowed down, but, now that he was no longer involved in concert promotion, he had the more time, and the continuing encouragement of his original backers, to devote to its preparation. His situation had elements of stability of which Ware would have recognised the value. But by the time Ware landed his chiroplast, his former apprentice's eyes were increasingly turned to Dublin. To St George's in the summer of 1819, on the occasion of a 'surplus collection at Mr Bunting's instance', he brought 'gentlemen of Christ Church and St Patrick's, Dublin to come and chaunt the service', and sing anthems and *Messiah* excerpts.[11] Also, he had become friendly with Mary Anne Chapman, whose mother ran a school in Belfast. When Mrs Chapman moved to Dublin and set up school there, her daughter went with her. On 20 January 1819, a bachelor of forty-five, Bunting wrote to Mrs Chapman asking for the hand of her daughter in marriage.[12] The marriage took place, and Edward Bunting left Belfast and lived the rest of his life in Dublin. After living for a time with Mrs Chapman, he and his wife set up house on their own in Upper Baggot Street. He writes to Mary Ann McCracken on 29 December 1820:

> I for the first time received the Sacrament at Patrick's Cathedral on Christmas Day with my lady. She seems happy now to what she did during her mother's superintendence of the household, in consequence of my altered behaviour perhaps. My little darling son [Anthony], she and I take the greatest delight in. He is grown handsome. All the people are delighted with him...[13]

*

Petrie covers the transition to the Irish metropolis, to a new career, and to a new life as a family man:

> Hitherto ... he had for a period of more than forty years been living at little cost with the respectable family of the McCrackens at Belfast, to whose house he had been invited when he arrived there at the age of eleven, 'getting and spending' as he pleased, but certainly not saving. He had now to commence house-keeping on his own account ... to earn his bread in a new locality, where he was comparatively little known, and where he would have to contend with professors of his art, of high powers and established reputations – and that at an advanced period of life, when the mind is as indisposed to form new friendships or associations, as the public is to reciprocate them. Yet he was not unsuccessful. Through the influence of his Northern connexions, he soon got into extensive practice as a teacher in the higher circles, and was appointed organist of St Stephen's chapel; and thus toiling daily and without rest, he was enabled to support a growing family in respectability, and had the happiness to leave them able, if required, by the exercise of their own talents to provide for themselves.[14]

His skills as solo pianist and concert promoter were not availed of in the higher reaches of Dublin musical life; at his age, as Petrie implies, it would be remarkable if they were. As an organist, he was highly regarded, but the two cathedrals were not available. In Christ Church and St Patrick's during his years in Dublin the posts of organist and choirmaster were in the hands of John Matthews, William Warren, Francis Robinson (Master Robinson of the 1813 festival) and his brother John; there was no way into that company for an outsider. In 1827, however, Bunting landed an excellent post. He wrote to Mary Ann McCracken:

> I received an unsought letter from the Trustees of Georges Church (where a new organ price £1,000 has been put up lately), to be their organist with a salary of from £90 to £100 a year, for which situation above twenty candidates started and canvassed the Parish... I am indebted for this place to the Attorney-General, who sent for me and spoke to me so kindly and friendly...[15]

The Attorney-General was Mary Ann McCracken's cousin, Henry Joy, who, as Fox says, 'shared the enthusiasm of his relatives for Irish music and antiquities'. The McCracken family had indeed done well by their old friend and one-time lodger. 'Georges Church' was Francis Johnston's Great St George's, opened in 1813 at the intersection of Temple Street and Hardwicke Street. It was a very fashionable quarter; Francis Johnston himself lived nearby in Eccles Street. It is a notable circumstance of Bunting's career as an organist that he played on so many new organs. Second Presbyterian was a new organ, as were those of both his St George's; indeed, the organ in St Anne's was only three years old when he came there to serve his apprenticeship.

Bunting kept links with Belfast, largely through the McCrackens. For several years before he left Belfast, the Irish Harp Society had not been doing well. By 1812 it was in financial trouble; Arthur O'Neill died in 1816 in his eighties after a spell in undeserved penury. Temporary rescue came from an unexpected quarter, when more than three hundred Ulstermen domiciled in Bengal, most of them army officers, made 'a liberal subscription ... for the revival of the harp'. A Belfast committee, including Bunting, was set up for the management of the 'India money'.[16] Nearly £1,200 was lodged, a former pupil, Valentine Rainey, was appointed tutor and the Society continued in existence. But by 1839, when Bunting wrote from Dublin for news of the Society, he got a doleful reply from the secretary, John McAdam:

> The funds will be exhausted about the 1st of February next. After the

> 1st of August we shall have only two boys; we are anxious to prolong the time, that one of the boys (William Murphy) may have as much instruction as can be afforded, he having his eyesight perfect, and a natural taste for music...We might probably keep up the Society for a few years longer by private subscription, but from the fact that the young harpers can only earn their bread by playing in hotels, where they are too liable to contract fatal habits, we think the money could be more usefully laid out in other charities. Our gentry in Ireland are too scarce, and too little national, to encourage itinerant harpers, as of old; besides, the taste and fashion of music no longer bears upon our national instrument: it had its day, but like all other fashions, it must give way to novelty.[17]

Busy man as he now was, Bunting never lost his commitment to the culminating volume of his collection of the ancient music. The energetic young researcher had slowed down a great deal, but in this field, in Dublin, he was among friends, notably George Petrie, and it was they who kept up the persuasion he needed. Petrie, commending the thoroughness and comprehensive nature of his approach to his material, says:

> We have reason to believe that while thus labouring he was not even sanguine in the hope that he should be able to do more than leave the work after him finished for better times, for he had little expectation that he should find a publisher.[18]

A publisher was found, and the third collection came out at last in 1840.[19] Edward Bunting died on 21 December 1843, aged seventy, and was buried in the cemetery of Mount Jerome in Dublin. This essay has shown, it is hoped, that Bunting's total career, in the mainstream music of his day and the nascent study of Irish traditional music, was all of a piece. There is never any indication, once he became involved in 'the ancient music', that he contemplated subordinating, much less abandoning, the one music for the other.

His personal character remains elusive. Petrie, we feel, has been content to take Bunting's own account of his earlier life, which is to be set against the view of his contemporary Mattie McTier. Petrie, however, no hagiographer, leaves us in no doubt that the older Bunting that he knew could be difficult to get on with:

> as his temper had been spoiled by indulgence and want of control in

> early life, it was sometimes necessary for his friends to bear a little with this infirmity[20]

and it has to be said that this is the curmudgeonly character strongly conveyed in the two portraits of him in later life, that in Fox and especially that in Petrie reproduced as the frontispiece in this book. The Brocas likeness is of a man midway between youth and old age; when it was taken its subject had the Catalani concerts and the second volume of the ancient music behind him and the 1813 festival ahead. The Bunting depicted there could patently age into the crusty old man of the later depictions; equally obviously, he has grown from a younger man who has put on weight and dignity. But it tells us very little of his face or his facial expression and it certainly gives no indication whatever of the explosive missionary energy which enabled Bunting to produce his pioneering first volume in four years. For William Ware, we need only the single portrait which exists. For Bunting the iconography cries out for completion. Petrie says he (the man he knew) was

> in size above the middle stature, and he was strongly made, and well proportioned. His somewhat English face was also symmetrical, and its expression manly and independent, full of intelligence and character, and must in youth have been eminently handsome.[21]

Surely, we feel, someone must have sketched the young apprentice organist, the teenage researcher?

Bunting in later life. Reproduced from a daguerreotype as the frontispiece in Charlotte Milligan Fox, *Annals of the Irish Harpers.*

NOTES

1 *BN-L*, 12 January 1816.
2 *BN-L*, 13 November 1802.
3 *BN-L*, 13 November 1808.
4 *BN-L*, 15 September 1809.
5 *BCC*, 16 August 1809.
6 *BN-L*, 13 September 1803.
7 *BN-L*, 10 May 1808.
8 *BCC*, 30 June 1811.
9 *BN-L*, 2 September 1815. Adroit publicity by Logier secured the success of the chiroplast in Britain, and it also reached Europe and the USA. One of its most attractive claims was that it enabled several pupils to be taught at once (one to one has always been the bogey of instrumental tuition). Much controversy was aroused, but some eminent pianists including Kalkbrenner adopted the idea, and Spohr defended it. Kalkbrenner's improved version was sold in England as late as 1877. The chiroplast has long disappeared.
10 Bunting in London to Mary Ann McCracken in Belfast, 1809, letter reproduced in NORMAN MCNEILLY, *The Music Makers* (Belfast, Linen Hall Library, 1976), p. 5.
11 *BN-L*, 6 July 1819.
12 FOX, *Annals*, p. 62.
13 FOX, *Annals*, p. 65.
14 PETRIE, *Bunting*, p. 72.
15 FOX, *Annals*, pp. 65-6.
16 *BN-L*, 4 May 1819.
17 BUNTING 1840, pp. 66-7.
18 PETRIE, *Bunting*, p. 72.
19 It is a sad irony that Petrie, so encouraging to Bunting, fared less well; of his own collection, one volume was published in his lifetime; an incomplete second was published posthumously.
20 PETRIE, *Bunting*, p. 73.
21 PETRIE, *Bunting*, p. 73.

APPENDIX 1

PROGRAMMES OF THE 1813 FESTIVAL

THESE PROGRAMMES are reproduced as reported in the *Belfast News-Letter* of 26 October, except for Bunting's benefit concert, the programme of which was advertised in advance in the *Belfast News-Letter* of 19 October. Information given between square brackets is editorial.

The first festival performance. A concert in the theatre on the evening of Tuesday 19 October 1813.

ACT 1

Grand overture, *Zaira*	Winter
Glee, 'When shall we three meet again?'	
Song, Mr Weyman, 'Blooming joys for ever new'	
Glee and chorus, 'Here in cool grot and mossy cell'	[Mornington]
Song, Mrs Cooke	Pucitta
Duett, Mr Spray and Miss Spray	
Glee, 'Foresters, sound the cheerful horn'	Bishop
Song, Miss Spray	Pucitta
Glee, five voices, 'When winds breathe soft along the silent deep'	Webbe

ACT II

Grand Overture, *Zauberflöte*	Mozart
Song, Mr Jager, 'I know a bank whereon the wild thyme grows' [newspaper report includes the words]	Percy
Concerto, flute, Mr Weidner	Weidner
Song, Mr T Cooke, 'Love unperceiv'd with cautious art', words by Miss Owenson	Cooke
Song, Mr Spray, 'The war that for a space did fail', [words, from Scott's *Marmion*, included in report]	Dr Clarke
Song, Mrs Cooke, accompanied on the trumpet by Mr H Willman [words, commencing 'I love, but I dare not say who', included in report]	Reeve
Sestetto, from *The Haunted Tower*, 'By mutual love delighted'	Storace

The second festival performance, in Dr Drummond's Meeting House on the morning of Wednesday 20 October.

PART I

Occasional Overture	Handel
Chorus, 'He gave them hailstones', *Israel in Egypt*	[Handel]
Song, Miss Spray, 'Praise the Lord ye heavenly Choir', *Esther* [*recte* 'Praise the Lord with cheerful noise']	Handel
Trio, 'Disdainful of danger', *Judas Maccabeus*	[Handel]
Song, Mr Jager, 'Return, O God of hosts' [*Samson*]	Handel
Chorus, 'O Father whose Almighty power' [*Judas Maccabeus*]	[Handel]
Song, Mrs Cooke, 'Angels ever bright and fair', *Judas Maccabeus* [*recte Theodora*]	[Handel]
Chorus, 'The horse and his rider', *Israel in Egypt*	[Handel]

PART II

Overture, with the Dead March, *Saul*	Handel
Song, Mr Weyman, 'Arm ye brave', *Judas Maccabeus*	[Handel]
Chorus, 'We come', *Judas Maccabeus*	[Handel]
Song, Mr Spray, 'Total eclipse', *Samson*	[Handel]
Chorus, 'O first created beam' [*Samson*]	[Handel]
Concerto Violin, Mr T Cooke	Viotti
Song, Mrs Cooke, 'Let the bright Seraphim' [*Samson*], accompanied on the trumpet by Mr H Willman	[Handel]
Chorus, 'Let their celestial concerts' [*Samson*]	Handel
Song, Master Robinson, 'Lord, what is man'	[Purcell]
Chorus, 'Coronation Anthem'	Handel
Finale, 'God save great George our King'.	

Bunting's benefit concert, on Wednesday evening 20 October in the theatre.

ACT I

Overture	Cooke
Glee, 'Hark, the lark at Heaven's Gate sings'	Cooke
Song, Mr Jager, 'The Maid of the Mountain'	Bishop
Glee and chorus, 'Hark the hollow woods'	Shield
Song, Master Robinson, 'Thou hast gone away from me, Mary'	
Song, Mrs Cooke, 'Sweet Robin'	Cooke
Concerto, trumpet, Mr Willman	Cooke
Song, Mr Spray, 'When for our laws and native land'	Stevenson
Finale, 'Viva Enrico'	Pucitta

ACT II

Concerto, violin, Mr T Cooke	Kreutzer
Glee, 'Oh! Nanny, wilt thou gang with me', harmonised by Harrison	
Song, Mrs Cooke	Pucitta
Military Concerto, pianoforte, Mr Bunting	Latour
Glee, 'See our bark', violin obbligato	Sir J Stevenson
Polacca, from *The Cabinet*, Mr Cooke	Braham
Duet, Messrs Spray and Weyman, 'Tell me, where is fancy bred'	Sir J Stevenson
Finale, 'Rule Britannia'	

The third festival performance, on Thursday morning 21 October in Dr Drummond's Meeting House.

PART I

A Selection from Haydn's celebrated Oratorio of *The Creation*

PART II

Concerto	Corelli
Song, Master Robinson, 'Pious orgies' [*Judas Maccabeus*] [words included in report]	Handel
Song, Mrs Cooke, 'Hymn of Eve' [*The Death of Abel*] [words included in report]	Dr Arne
Song [*recte* Recitative], Mr Spray, 'Deeper and deeper still' [*Jephtha*] [words included in report]	Handel
Chorus, 'Fixed in his everlasting seat'	Handel
Song, Miss Spray, 'What tho' I trace', *Solomon*	[Handel]
Concerto, flute, Mr Weidner	Weidner
Song [*recte* Recitative], Mr Jager, 'Thou shalt bring them in' [words included in report]	Handel
Chorus, *Coronation Anthem*	Handel

The fourth festival performance, a concert on Thursday evening 21 October in the theatre.

ACT 1

Overture	Winter
Glee, 'Red Cross Knights'	Dr Calcott
Song, Mr Jager, with violin obbligato, 'Where were ye, nymphs'	Stevenson
Duet, Mr and Miss Spray, 'Ye banks and braes'	
Concerto on the new patent Kent bugle, Mr H Willman	Cooke
Song, Mr Spray, 'O'er Nelson's tomb'	
Song, Mrs Cooke, 'Sweet maid'	Bishop
Trio, 'The flocks shall leave the mountains' [*Acis and Galatea*]	Handel

ACT II

Symphony	Haydn
Song, Mr Weyman, 'The wolf'	Shield
Duet, Mr and Mrs Cooke, 'Il tuo destine ingrata'	Portogallo
Glee, 'Life's a bumper'	Wainwright
Rondo, violin, Mr T Cooke	Viotti
Song, Miss Spray, 'O quando amore'	Pucitta
Glee, 'With the sun'	Stevenson
Song, Mr Cooke, 'Spirit of my sainted sire' [*The Haunted Tower*]	Storace
Song, Mrs Cooke, 'Little blind boy'	Kelly
Air, Mr Spray, 'Come if you dare'	Purcell
Chorus, 'We come'	Purcell

The fifth performance, Handel's *Messiah*, on Friday morning 22 October in Dr Drummond's Meeting House.

The programme of the Bunting performance is transcribed verbatim as reported in the *Belfast News-Letter* of 26 October, alongside the numbered order of pieces in the familiar present-day Novello piano-and-vocal edition edited by H Watkins Shaw. Those numbers in Watkins Shaw which do not appear in Bunting, and presumably were not performed, have been italicised. Information between square brackets is editorial.

BUNTING	WATKINS SHAW	
PART I	PART ONE	
Overture	1 Sinfonia (Overture)	
Recitative, accompanied, Mr Spray, 'Comfort ye, comfort ye my people, saith your God'	2 'Comfort ye my people'	Recit.
Song, [Mr Spray] 'Every valley'	3 'Ev'ry valley shall be exalted'	Air
Chorus, 'And the glory of the Lord shall be revealed'	4 'And the glory of the Lord'	Chorus
Recitative, accompanied, Mr Weyman, 'Thus saith the Lord of Hosts'	5 'Thus saith the Lord'	Recit.
Air [Mr Weyman?] 'But who may abide the day of his coming?'	6 'But who may abide the day of his coming?'	Air
	7 'And he shall purify'	*Chorus*
Recitative, Mr Jager, 'Behold a virgin shall conceive, and bear a son, and shall call his name Emanuel'	8 'Behold, a virgin shall conceive'	Recit.
Song [Mr Jager] and Chorus, 'O thou that tellest tidings to Zion'	9 'O thou that tellest good tidings to Zion'	Air and Chorus

Handel's *Messiah*, continued

BUNTING	WATKINS SHAW	
Recitative, accompanied, Mr Weyman, 'For behold, darkness shall cover the earth, and gross darkness the people'	10 'For behold, darkness shall cover the earth'	Recit.
Song [Mr Weyman] 'The people that walked in darkness'	11 'The people that walked in darkness'	Air
Chorus, 'For unto us a Child is born'	12 'For unto us a child is born'	Chorus
	13 Pifa ('Pastoral Symphony')	
Recitative, Master Robinson, 'There were shepherds abiding in the field, keeping watch over their flocks by night'	14 (a) 'There were shepherds abiding in the field'	Recit.
[Master Robinson?]	(b) 'And lo, the angel of the Lord came upon them'	Recit.
[Master Robinson?]	15 'And the angel said unto them'	Recit.
[Master Robinson?]	16 'And suddenly there was with the angel'	Recit.
Chorus, 'Glory to God in the highest'	17 'Glory to God'	Chorus
Song, Miss Spray, 'Rejoice greatly, O daughters of Zion'	18 'Rejoice greatly, O daughter of Zion'	Air
	19 '*Then shall the eyes of the blind*'	Recit.
Song, Mr Spray, 'Come unto him all ye that labour'	20 '*He shall feed his flock*'	Air
Song (introduced), Mrs Cooke, 'Farewell ye limpid streams' (from *Jephtha*), [*recte* 'Farewell, ye limpid springs and floods']		
	21 'His yoke is easy, and his burthen is light'	*Chorus*

Handel's *Messiah*, continued

BUNTING	WATKINS SHAW	
	PART TWO	
	22 'Behold the Lamb of God'	*Chorus*
Song, Mr Jager, 'He was despised and rejected of men'	23 'He was despised'	Air
	24 'Surely he hath borne our griefs'	*Chorus*
	25 'And with his stripes we are healed'	*Chorus*
Chorus, 'All we like sheep have gone astray'	26 'All we like sheep have gone astray'	Chorus

End of PART I

In the interval,

Concerto, organ, Mr Bunting, Corelli's 11th

PART II

BUNTING	WATKINS SHAW	
Recitative, accompanied, Mr Spray, 'All they that see him laugh him to scorn'	27 'All they that see him laugh him to scorn'	Recit.
Chorus, 'He trusted in God that he would deliver him'	28 'He trusted in God'	Chorus
Recitative, accompanied, Mr Spray, 'Thy rebuke hath broken his heart; he is full of heaviness'	29 'Thy rebuke hath broken his heart'	Recit.
Song [Mr Spray] 'Behold and see if there be any sorrow like unto his sorrow'	30 'Behold, and see if there be any sorrow'	Air
Recitative, accompanied, Miss Spray, 'He was cut off out of the land of the living'	31 'He was cut off out of the land of the living'	Recit.
Song, Miss Spray, 'But thou didst not leave his soul in hell; nor didst thou suffer thy Holy one to see corruption'	32 'But thou didst not leave his soul in hell'	Air
Semi-chorus, 'Lift up your heads, O! ye gates'	33 'Lift up your heads, O ye gates'	Chorus

Handel's *Messiah*, continued

BUNTING	WATKINS SHAW	
Chorus, 'The Lord of Hosts; he is the King of Glory'		
	**34 'Unto which of the angels said he at any time'*	*Recit.*
	**35 'Let all the angels of God worship him'*	*Chorus*
	**36 'Thou art gone up on high'*	*Air*
	37 'The Lord gave the word'	*Chorus*
	38 'How beautiful are the feet'	*Air*
	39 'Their sound is gone out'	*Chorus*
Song, Mr Weyman, 'Why do the nations so furiously rage?'	40 'Why do the nations so furiously rage together?'	Air
	41 'Let us break their bonds asunder'	*Chorus*
	42 'He that dwelleth in heaven'	*Recit.*
	43 'Thou shalt break them'	*Air*
	44 'Hallelujah'	Chorus
	PART THREE	
Chorus, 'Worthy is the Lamb'	see 53 below	
Song, Master Robinson, 'I know that my Redeemer liveth'	45 'I know that my Redeemer liveth'	Air
Chorus, 'Since by man came death'	46 'Since by man came death'	Chorus
Recitative, accompanied, Mr Weyman 'Behold, I tell you a mystery'	47 'Behold, I tell you a mystery'	Recit.
Song, [Mr Weyman], accompanied by Mr H Willman, 'The trumpet shall sound, and the dead shall be raised'	48 'The trumpet shall sound'	Air
	**49 'Then shall be brought to pass'*	*Recit.*
	**50 'O death, where is thy sting'*	*Duet*

Handel's *Messiah*, continued

BUNTING	WATKINS SHAW	
	**51 'But thanks be to God'*	*Chorus*
Song, Mr Spray, 'If God be for us'	*52 'If God be for us'	Air
	53 'Worthy is the Lamb that was slain'	Chorus
	[see above on left]	
Chorus, 'Hallelujah! for the Lord God omnipotent reigneth' [see 44 above]		

APPENDIX II

From the *Belfast News-Letter*
20, 23 November 1813:

CRITICAL REMARKS ON THE LATE MUSICAL FESTIVAL IN BELFAST

Written on the probability of its being occasionally repeated.

(The remainder of the following paper, containing (besides a conclusion of the critique on the performance) the author's opinion of the plan which it would be advisable to act upon on future festivals, is unavoidably postponed till our next.)

[Paragraph 1]

To the same source that we are indebted for those beautiful remains of Gothic *architecture*, with its majestic ranges of cluster'd columns, and its 'high embowed roofs,' we owe THE ORATORIO; a species of music peculiarly suited in its peformance in such extensive structures. To the awful impressions of religion we may also trace the greatest productions in *Painting*, and the most elevated flight of English *Poetry*, Paradise Lost.

[Para. 2]

The origin of Oratorios has been attributed to the Crusaders, on their return from the Holy Land. In their present improved state, they comprehend almost all that is grand and pathetic in Music. In so much, that, however correct and chaste his native taste may be, he who has not heard of Oratorio has but a faint idea of the power of one of the finest of the fine arts. He does not even know the perfection to which *simple melody*, or the succession of single sounds, can be carried under the direction of genius. He would be surprised to find how perfectly the plainest airs can be made to assimilate with all that is sublime and beautiful; and of the chorus, it is impossible he should have formed an adequate conception. It was natural, therefore, that a professor of music, of the first character, and amateurs, who had enjoyed such treats elsewhere, should have desired to introduce an entertainment, calculated to charm every ear, and to excite musical taste in a district where it never flourished.

[Para. 3]

With respect to the recent experiment, it may safely be asserted that, considering it a novel one, in which numerous difficulties presented themselves (particularly in the prospect of very prescribed means*) our late Festival was brought out with a degree of correctness and effect, that no one expected, and that none had a right to expect; especially as it was on a scale not aimed at even in the capital of this kindgom, since Handel took refuge in it from the erroneous taste of an English Nobility.

[Para. 4]

Observations on the performances are now offered; with due respect for the professional gentlemen, of whose practical abilities they gave ample proofs. As the object of such music is to make suitable impressions on the public mind, those to whom it is addressed may of right claim the liberty of declaring, in what points those ends have been accomplished, and, in what in any degree, they may have fallen short.

THEATRE – EVENING CONCERT, OCT. 19.

[Para. 5]

This consisted chiefly of two Overtures, by Winter, and Mozart, with a number of songs and glees. Among the best of the latter was Lord Mornington's celebrated one, 'Here in cool grot and mossy cell'; of the songs, that taken from *Marmion*, 'The war that for a space did fall'. The entire selection of this evening was good, and the execution of it would have had an excellent effect in a *music room*; but the theatre of this town is so ill calculated for vocal performances, that it was regretted that more of the three evenings entertainments were not devoted to *instrumental* music, the band being powerful, harmonious, and complete.

SECOND EVENING CONCERT.

[Para. 6]

The objection on the theatre was even more obvious this night, than the preceding. The beautiful glee, 'Hark, the lark at heav'n's gate sings', given by Mr. Cooke, &c. and the simple air, 'Thou hast gone awa' from me, Mary,' by Master Robinson, of the choir of Christ Church, were heard to little advantage. Not so the spirit-stirring *Trumpet Concerto*, by Willman, which conquered every defect of the house. In Mr T. Cooke's Violin Concerto, from the cause before mentioned, the attentive audience could perceive only great execution, while the delicate finger of the performer was nearly lost. Mr Bunting's Military Concerto shared the same fate, though it received great applause from the performers themselves, who were within hearing of it.

THIRD EVENING'S CONCERT.

[Para. 7]

Mr Willman's Concerto on the patent bugle was deservedly admired, and well heard; while Handel's sweet Trio, from *Acis and Galatea*, 'The flocks shall leave the mountains', though excellently sung, produced little effect.

MORNING PERFORMANCES.

[Para. 8]

The MORNING'S were dedicated to *Sacred* compositions, in Dr. Drummond's meeting-house, where all the powers of a very numerous band were fully exerted. They had there the aid of a very fine organ, touched by the masterly finger of Mr Bunting, whose talents were even more admired by his professional associates, than by those who have been in the habit of experiencing them. The arrangement of so great a number of performers, and an assemblage of the first

Nobility and Gentry in Ulster, produced a *coup d'oeil* at once noble and interesting.

FIRST MORNING – OCT. 20

[Para. 9]
Was devoted to a Miscellaneous Concert, chiefly from the works of HANDEL. The great majority of a crowded audience witnessed, for the first time, the astonishing powers of that great composer, in the chorus from *Israel in Egypt*, 'He gave them hailstones', followed by the Trio from *Judas Maccabeus*, 'Disdainful of danger', by the ecstatic strain 'Angels ever bright and fair', and by the Chorus from *Israel in Egypt*, 'The horse and his rider', &c.

[Para. 10]
The second act opened with Handel's overture in *Saul*, comprehending the Dead March, which has never been equalled. It is hardly conceivable, that any combination of instruments could give greater interest to that solemn movement. As performed, it in truth answered to Milton's exquisite lines:

At last a soft and solemn breathing sound
Rose like a steam of rich distill'd perfume,
And stole upon the air.

In 'Total eclipse', from *Sampson*, Mr. Spray threw the happiest emphasis on the words 'no sun – no moon – all dark amid the blaze of noon! Sun, moon, and stars are dark to me!' It was the lot of both Handel and Milton, from whose *Sampson Agonistes* the passage was taken, to be deprived of sight in the vale of years; and with the truest pathos have they, in their respective lines, deplored its loss. Master Robinson was admired in the air, 'What is man'. But nothing could excel the song which was sung by Mrs Cooke, accompanied by the silver tones of Mr. Willman's trumpet, which gave equal surprize and delight:

Let the bright Seraphim in burning Row,

Their loud uplifted angel-trumpets blow;
Let the cherubic host, in tuneful choirs,
Touch their immortal harps with golden wires.

The three choruses, 'We come', from *Judas Maccabeus*, 'O first created beam', 'Let their celestial concerts', and the Coronation Anthem, were excellently performed. A Violin Concerto (Viotti) by Mr. T. Cooke, displayed the greatest command of that noble instrument.

SECOND MORNING.

[Para. 11]

An opportunity was this day afforded of ascertaining the comparative merits of our modern composer, Haydn, with those of Handel, in the composition of an Oratorio. After the impression left in the former morning by some of the exalted strains of the latter, most of the auditors found little difficulty in forming a determination. Nothing could have been more nobly conceived than the subject of Haydn's *Creation*, had a representation of that subject come within the compass of human genius. But that stupendous event, which has ever set at nought the researches of the philosopher, and to which every thing, except divine poetry itself, has proved inadequate, was not to be described in musical sounds. For a description equal to the theme, we must content ourselves with that book from which Longinus takes the truest example of the sublime, in the passage 'Let there be light! and there was light'; and for the finest paraphrase of it with the 7th book of Milton's immortal work, in which the sublimity of the original sinks into the beautiful. But in Haydn's *musical* attempt we seek for it in vain.

[Para. 12]

The great master of his art seems better to have known its limits: Handel aimed at objects which he perfectly attained; strains exquisitely expressive of devout feelings; of praise to God from single voices, heightened by delicate touches of instrumental harmony; or bursting forth in all the majesty of the chorus. Haydn is unrivalled in the art of adapting the greatest number, and the greatest variety of instruments, to their respective parts; and by giving full employment to each, of making every performer in the band sensible of his own importance; a circumstance to which it is partly owing that musicians are apt to prefer him to the elder composers. But it was the glory of Handel's compositions, by bold strokes to storm the heart, to agitate every nerve in our frame, to melt us down to the most tender melancholy, or to excite the most cheerful hopes of a state of future bliss. The selection from the *Creation* was followed by different airs and choruses from Handel, and by a flute concerto by Mr. Weidner. Excellently as the last was executed it must be remarked that performers too seldom employ their powers in simple airs, in which their *taste* would delight more than their waste of execution astonishes. This applies also to Mr. Cooke's admirable performance on the violin. With all respect to their better judgment, the observation is worth their notice, that 'it is not in performing difficulties that the beautiful consists, and that sooner or later nature *will* prevail'.

To be concluded in our next.

[Para. 13]

* *Note* – How limited those means were, may be conceived from the fund raised in other places for similar purposes. The late Liverpool Festival produced, by a *Sermon*, with which it opened, £300 – *Tickets* for its five performances produced £4,500 – A Ball, £1,250 and a donation from one of its Members in Parliament, £50, making an aggregate of *£6,050!*, near one-third of which went to charitable funds. The number of Subscribers was 1,250. Persons at one time in the ballroom, 2,228.

CRITICAL REMARKS ON THE LATE MUSICAL FESTIVAL IN BELFAST

Written on the probability of its being occasionally repeated.
(Concluded from our last.)

FRIDAY MORNING – THE MESSIAH.

[Para. 14]

We have now reached the concluding day's amusement of this delightful week, which took for its *finale* the greatest production of HANDEL; the offspring of his genius at an advanced period of life, when that of many others would have been exhausted, which in him appeared to gain fresh vigour as he approached his end. No composition, taken as a whole, has ever come in competition with it. The selections of the preceding days gave general satisfaction, and most in proportion as they were drawn from *his* works; but this Oratorio afforded a regular and unfailing source of delight – 'a sober certainty of waking bliss', from beginning to end. 'Comfort ye, my people' has long been held the best recitative that was ever produced. The well known air, 'I know that my Redeemer liveth, and that he shall stand at the latter day upon the earth: and though worms destroy this body, yet in my flesh shall I see God. For now is Christ risen from the dead, the first fruits of them that sleep', probably rises to 'the highest heaven' of musical invention; to its greatest pitch of sublimity and pathos. His only other song which seems to have been inspired by similar feelings is 'Angels ever bright and fair', in which Master Robinson's voice, sweet as it is, wanted that firmness of tone which every air of Handel's requires. 'He was despised and rejected of men, a man of sorrow, and acquainted with grief', was given with delicacy and feeling by Mr. Jager; and the air, 'Farewell ye limpid streams', introduced from *Jephtha*, and sung by Mrs. Cooke, was extremely admired.

[Para. 15]

The choruses in the first act were performed with great spirit, and in true harmony. That of 'For unto us a child is born; unto us a Son is given; and the government shall be upon his shoulder; and his name shall be called WONDERFUL – COUNSELLOR – THE MIGHTY GOD – the Everlasting Father – the Prince of Peace', left such an impression on the memory of a crowded intelligent audience, as many years cannot efface.

[Para. 16]

To enumerate the exquisite airs that adorn the piece, were to mention them all; for a collection equally rich and excellent throughout, is not to be found in musical annals. Whether in the songs or the choruses, the genius of Handel here displayed itself in its utmost grandeur. Succeeding composers have endeavoured to imitate and rival them, but in vain. He must have understood our language sufficiently to enter into the spirit of the English version of the Scriptures, some of the most sublime passages in which he has taken for his purpose. Few finer examples could be given of descriptive poetry than the following, from *Paradise Lost*; which we might be tempted to think influenced him in some of his sacred compositions. He appears, indeed, to have had a predilection even for the lighter poems of Milton, having set his song 'Let me wander not unseen', and both *L'Allegro* and *Il Penseroso* to music.

Then crown'd again, their golden harps they took,
Harps ever tun'd, that glittering by their side
Like quivers hung, and with preamble sweet
Of charming symphony, they introduce
Their sacred song, and waken raptures high.

*

How often from the steep
Of echoing hill or thicket have we heard
Celestial voices to the midnight air,
Sole, or responsive each to others note,
Singing their great Creator? Oft in bands
While they keep watch, or nightly rounding walk,
With heav'nly touch of instrumental sounds

In full harmonic number joined, their songs
Divide the night, and lift our thoughts to Heaven.

THE CHORUS

No sooner had th' Almighty ceased, but all
The multitude of Angels, with a shout
Loud as from numbers without number, sweet
As from blest voices, uttering joy, Heav'n rung
With jubilee, and loud Hosannas fill'd
Th' eternal regions: lowly reverent
Tow'rds either throne they bow and to the ground,
With solemn adoration, down they cast
Their crowns inwove with amarant and gold.

The transcendent excellence of Handel is not at this day to be questioned; nearly a century has confirmed it. In the words of Dr. Browne, it may safely be asserted that 'upon the whole, his *airs, duets and choirs*, as they surpass every thing yet produced, in grandeur and expression; so they will ever be the richest fountain for imitation or adoption; and even singly taken, will justly command the regard and admiration of all succeeding ages'.

[Para. 17]

It remains to make a few observations on the plan of the late Festival, in the expectation of a future one.

[Para. 18]

It has been already noticed, that *Cathedrals* are most appropriate to such entertainments; and it is offered as the opinion of an Individual, that situated as we are, the Parish Church of Belfast, with its organ in good order, would, on different accounts, be preferable for this purpose to other places of worship. The Festival might, in that case, commence with a *sermon*, by a dignitary of the establishment, for the sole benefit of the poor; the propriety of which may be estimated by the collection on a similar occasion at Liverpool.

[Para. 19]

The *time*, when a repetition of the Festival should take place, seems to determine itself; either immediately on the breaking up of the great musical meetings in England, or on the occasional visits of the best singers to our Irish metropolis. On such occasions, one or two of the first rate singers that our sister country affords might be procured on moderate terms. The value even of ONE supereminent voice, and the beneficial effect it would have on the receipts, are obvious.

[Para. 20]

The principal object in view, is the promotion of charity, blended with elegant, rational amusement; obtained on the best terms, and with least trouble to the Inhabitants. It is therefore suggested, that a single individual should take future Festivals at his own risque, with an ultimate view of deriving profit from them. The express terms to be, that a certain proportion of *the sales of tickets* (not of net profits) shall go to the use of *the poor*: say 25 or 30 per cent, including those issued for a ball on Monday, and a ball and supper on Friday. By this plan, one person would have an interest in carrying it into effect in the best manner; securing such vocal and instrumental performers as would ensure him success; rejecting those non effectives that generally attach themselves to great music meetings; and studying a prudent economy in every thing. The necessary strength of the choral band he would carefully consider, so as not to have it unnecessarily numerous, nor clogged by tame inanimate voices, but suited to the capaciousness of the house.

[Para. 21]

It ought also, to form part of the agreement, that the chief singers, and principal instrumental performers, be announced before any tickets are issued, at least a month preceding it; in order that the entertainment to be expected, may be early ascertained.

[Para. 22]

It is questionable whether the *Theatre* ought not to be dropt for Evening Concerts, being so ill calculated for them, substituting the elegant centre room in the *Exchange*, with the addition, if found requisite, of the two smaller rooms. Without these last, 300 auditors could, it is thought, be accommodated with perfect convenience.

[Para. 23]

It will deserve consideration, whether, in case our future bands be as numerous and complete as the last, more time ought not to be devoted to *instrumental pieces*, in the evening meetings, with a due intermixture of vocal. Different tastes would be thus better accommodated. An important question arises, respecting the propriety of making a distinction of ranks, in the appropriation of certain boxes (in case the Theatre be still made use of). It was probably useful to make such distinction, in the extent it was, at the late Festival; at the same time that it appeared to be attended with much trouble and productive of some confusion. To extend the courtesy beyond moderate bounds in future, would seem ineligible. Perhaps it would answer a good purpose, were the distinction not to descend below the rank of Baronetage, Dignitaries of the Church to be an exception. Not more seats to be kept than tickets are purchased for; and those to be considered as vacant, if not occupied within an hour of the commencement of the concert.

[Para. 24]

Regulations of this kind, and others, for the general purpose of order, in and out of doors, and for financial arrangements, to be settled by Stewards, nominated by the Committee of the Belfast Charitable Society.

[Para. 25]

These remarks are probably, in different points, erroneous. They are thrown out in the hope that the subject will be early taken into consideration; and future Festivals conducted on some permanent principle, likely to ensure their continuance.

[Para. 26]

The glees at supper were ill managed; in future they might be given at intervals between the dancing sets in the great room.

BELFAST, NOV. 18, 1813.

[Para. 27]

☞ In England, Dignitaries of the Church encouraged the performance of Oratorios. Not one Reverend Bishop graced the Festival at Belfast.

[Para. 28]

Note. – The second act of the *Messiah* was preceded by the *eleventh concerto by Corelli*, on the Organ, by Mr Bunting. To the luxuriant playfulness, the fine harmony, and 'the native wood-notes wild', of that admired author, the organist did great justice.

BIBLIOGRAPHY

JEAN AGNEW (ed.), *The Drennan-McTier letters*, (3 volumes, Dublin, The Women's History Project in association with Irish Manuscripts Commission, 1998–9).

JONATHAN BARDON, *Belfast: an illustrated history* (Belfast, Blackstaff Press, 1982).

BEATH MSS, held in the Linen Hall Library.

J.C. BECKETT et al, *Belfast: the making of the city 1800–1914* (Belfast, Appletree Press, 1983).

'BELFASTIENSIS' (ISAAC WARD), 'Old Belfast: William Ware, the First Organist of the Parish Church, Belfast', in *Belfast Evening Telegraph*, 6 October 1898.

Belfast Literary Journal (Belfast, 1816).

GEORGE BENN, *The history of the town of Belfast* (Belfast, Mackay 1823).

JOHN BERNARD, *Retrospections of the stage* (2 volumes, London, H. Colburn and R. Bentley, 1830).

BRIAN BOYDELL, *Rotunda music in eighteenth-century Dublin* (Dublin, Irish Academic Press, 1992).

BREANDÁN BREATHNACH, *Folk music and dances of Ireland* (Cork, Mercier Press, 1971, revised edition 1977).

C.E.B. BRETT, *Buildings of Belfast* (revised edition, Belfast, Friar's Bush Press, 1985).

EDWARD BUNTING:

General Collection / of the / ANCIENT IRISH MUSIC / Containing a variety of / Admired Airs / never before Published and also / The Compositions of / CONALAN and CAROLAN / Collected from the Harpers &c in the different / Provinces of / IRELAND, / and adapted for the / Piano-Forte, with a Prefatory Introduction / by / EDWARD BUNTING / Vol. 1 (London, Preston, 1796).

A General / Collection of the ancient / MUSIC OF IRELAND, / Arranged for the / Piano Forte; / some of the most admired melodies are adapted for the Voice, /

To Poetry chiefly translated from the / Original Irish Songs, by / Thomas Campbell Esqr. / and / OTHER Eminent POETS: / To which is prefixed / A / Historical and Critical Dissertation / on / The Egyptian, British and / Irish Harp / by EDWARD BUNTING. / Vol. 1st. (London, Clementi & Co, 1809).

THE / ANCIENT MUSIC / of / IRELAND, / Arranged for the Pianoforte. / To which is prefixed / A DISSERTATION ON / THE IRISH HARP AND HARPERS, / including an account of the / OLD MELODIES OF IRELAND. / BY EDWARD BUNTING. (Dublin, Hodges & Smith, 1840).

BUNTING MSS, held in Queen's University Library, Belfast.

DAVID BYERS, *Belfast Musical Festival, 1813*, www.btinternet.com/~david.byers/homepage.htm.

The Manuscripts and Correspondence of James, first Earl of Charlemont 1745–99 (2 volumes, London, Historical Manuscripts Commission, 1891, 1894).

Christ Church Chapter Acts, September 1809 – January 1818 (Representative Church Body, C/6/1/7/9, 208).

WILLIAM SMITH CLARK, *The Irish stage in the county towns 1720 to 1800* (Oxford, Clarendon Press, 1963).

DEREK COLLINS, *Concert life in Dublin in the age of revolution* (unpublished PhD thesis, Queen's University Belfast, 2001).

HORTON DAVIES, *Worship and Theology in England* (5 volumes, Princeton, Princeton University, 1961–75).

Dictionary of National Biography (63 volumes, London, Smith, Elder, 1885–1900).

CYRIL EHRLICH, *The piano: a history* (revised edition, Oxford, Clarendon Press, 1990).

First Presbyterian Church: Congregational Minute Books 1760 – held in the church.

ALOIS FLEISCHMANN (ed.), *Music in Ireland: a Symposium* (Cork University Press and Blackwell, Oxford, 1952).

PETER FROGGATT, 'Dr James McDonnell, M.D., 1763–1845', *The Glynns: Journal of the Glens of Antrim Historical Society*, volume 9 (Impact Printing, Ballycastle,1981).

CHARLOTTE MILLIGAN FOX, *The annals of the Irish Harper*s (London, Smith, Elder, 1911).

ALEXANDER GORDON, *Historic memorials of the First Presbyterian Church of Belfast* (Belfast, Marcus Ward, 1887).

JOHN GRAY and WESLEY McCANN (eds), *An uncommon bookman: essays in memory of J.R.R. Adams* (Belfast, Linen Hall Library, 1996).

W.H. GRINDLE, *Irish cathedral music: a history of music at the cathedrals of the Church of Ireland* (Institute of Irish Studies, Queen's University Belfast, 1989).

HANDEL:

Messiah: ed. EBENEZER PROUT (London, Novello, 1902, and revised edition 1942).

Messiah: ed. WATKINS SHAW (Sevenoaks, Novello, 1962).

DAVID HARKNESS and MARY O'DOWD (eds), *The town in Ireland* (Belfast, Appletree Press, 1981).

ITA HOGAN, *Anglo-Irish music 1780–1830* (Cork, Cork University Press, 1966).

ROY JOHNSTON:

Concerts in the musical life of Belfast to 1874 (unpublished PhD thesis, Queen's University Belfast, 1996).

'The pleasures and penalties of networking: John Frederick Lampe in the summer of 1750', in SIMON McVEIGH and SUSAN WOLLENBERG (eds), *Concert life in eighteenth-century Britain* (Aldershot, Ashgate, forthcoming [2004]).

JOHN KILLEN, *A history of the Linen Hall Library 1788–1988* (Belfast, Linen Hall Library, 1990).

JOE McKEE, *The choral foundation of Armagh Cathedral 1600–1870*, (unpublished MA thesis, Queen's University Belfast, 1982).

NORMAN McNEILLY, *The Music Makers* (Belfast, Linen Hall Library, 1976).

SIMON McVEIGH:

The violinist in London's concert life 1750–84 (New York, Garland, 1989).

Concert life in London from Mozart to Haydn (Cambridge, Cambridge University Press, 1993).

JOHN MAGEE, *The heritage of the harp: the Linen Hall Library and the preservation of Irish music* (Belfast, Linen Hall Library 1992).

S. SHANNON MILLIN, *History of the Second Congregation of Presbyterian Dissenters in Belfast* (Belfast, Baird, 1900).

Minutes of Second Presbyterian Church, Belfast, held in the Public Record Office of Northern Ireland.

Minutes of the Irish Harp Society, held in the Linen Hall Library.

COLETTE MOLONEY, *The Irish music manuscripts of Edward Bunting (1773–1843): an introduction and catalogue* (Dublin, Irish Traditional Music Archive, 2000).

HAMILTON MOORE, *The young Gentleman and Ladies MONITOR, being a collection of select pieces from our modern writers: particularly calculated to form the mind and manners of the youth of both sexes, and adapted to the use of schools and academies, by Hamilton Moore, Esq. Used in the Academy, Belfast* (Belfast, James Magee, 1788), p. 284.

W.T. PARKE, *Musical memoirs* (2 volumes, London, Colburn and Bentley, 1830).

GEORGE PETRIE:

'Our portrait gallery. No XLI – Edward Bunting. With an etching,' in *Dublin University Magazine,* XXIX (clxix), (Dublin: James M'Glashan, and W.S. Orr, London, 1847). Signed 'P'.

The Petrie Collection of the Ancient Music of Ireland (Dublin, Dublin University Press, 1855).

RICHARD PINE and CHARLES ACTON, (eds), *To talent alone: the Royal Irish Academy of Music 1848–1998* (Dublin, Gill and Macmillan, 1998).

BRIAN PRITCHARD, *The Musical Festival and the Choral Society in England in the 18th and 19th centuries: a social history* (unpublished PhD thesis, Birmingham University, 1966).

BERNARR RAINBOW, *The land without music* (London, Novello, 1967).

MALCOLM RUTHVEN, *Belfast Philharmonic Society 1874–1974: a short history* (Belfast, 1974).

DAVID STEERS, '"An admirable finger directed by pure taste": Edward Bunting and Belfast's Second Presbyterian Congregation', *Bulletin of the Presbyterian Historical Society of Ireland,* 25, 1996, pp. 22–29.

A.T.Q. STEWART, *The Summer Soldiers: the 1798 Rebellion in Antrim and Down* (Belfast, Blackstaff Press, 1995).

NICHOLAS TEMPERLEY:

The music of the English parish church (2 volumes, Cambridge, Cambridge University Press, 1979).

Haydn: The Creation (Cambridge Music Handbooks, Cambridge University Press, 1991).

H.M. THOMPSON and F.J. BIGGER, *The Cathedral Church of Belfast* (Belfast, Baird, 1925).

Six anthems performed in Hillsborough Church: the music composed by Michael Thomson, Mus. D. (Hillsborough, 1786).

MRS ANNA WALKER, *Diary 1802–7*, held in the Public Record Office of Northern Ireland.

BRIAN M. WALKER and HUGH DIXON, *In Belfast town 1864–1880* (Belfast, Friar's Bush Press, 1984).

T.J. WALSH, *Opera in Dublin 1798–1820* (Oxford, Oxford University Press, 1993).

WILLIAM WARE:

Easy Instructions for the Piano Forte … carefully selected for facilitating the Improvement of Young Pupils (Dublin, Rhames, 1803, 2nd edition 1808).

Sacred harmony: a selection of psalm tunes, ancient and modern hymns and solo anthems (Dublin, Powers, 1809).

WILLIAM WEBER, *The rise of musical classics in 18th-century England: a study in canon, ritual and ideology* (Oxford, Clarendon Press, 1992).

GRAINNE YEATS, *The harp of Ireland* (Belfast, Belfast Harpers' Bicentenary, 1992).

R.M. YOUNG, *Historical notices of Old Belfast* (Belfast, Marcus Ward, 1896).

NEWSPAPERS

Belfast Commercial Chronicle – BCC (1805–1855)

Belfast Evening Telegraph – BET (1870–1918), continuing as *Belfast Telegraph* (1918 – present day)

Belfast Mercury or Freeman's Chronicle – BM (1783–1786), continuing as *Belfast Evening Post* (1786–1787)

Belfast News-Letter – BN-L (1737 – present day)

Faulkner's Dublin Journal

Northern Star – NS (1792–1797)

OTHER TITLES IN THE BELFAST NATURAL HISTORY AND PHILOSOPHICAL SOCIETY PUBLICATION SERIES

NO 1 *Equiano and anti-slavery in eighteenth-century Belfast*
Nini Rodgers
ISBN 0-9539604-0-4 £5.00

NO 2 *Double traitors?*
The Belfast Volunteers and Yeomen 1778–1828
Allan Blackstock
ISBN 0-9539604-1-2 £5.00

NO 3 *The time of the end*
Millenarian beliefs in Ulster
Myrtle Hill
ISBN 0-9539604-2-0 £5.00

NO 4 *H.B. Phillips, Impresario*
The man who brought McCormack, Kreisler and Robeson to Derry
Wesley McCann
ISBN 0-9539604-4-7 £7.00

NO 5 *An unlikely success story:*
The Belfast shipbuilding industry
J.P. Lynch
ISBN 0-9539604-3-9 £10.00

NO 6 *Captain Cahonny:*
Constantine Maguire of Tempo 1777–1834
W.A. Maguire
ISBN 0-9539604-5-5 £10.00